OTHER WORKS BY DAVID BUDBILL

POETRY

Why I Came to Judevine
From Down to the Village
The Chain Saw Dance
Barking Dog

PLAYS

Thingy World!
Judevine: The Play in Two Acts
Pulp Cutters' Nativity
Knucklehead Rides Again
Mannequins' Demise

SHORT STORIES

Snowshoe Trek to Otter River

NOVELS

Bones on Black Spruce Mountain

CHILDREN'S BOOKS

Christmas Tree Farm

JUDEVINE

The Complete Poems
1970–1990

DAVID BUDBILL

Chelsea Green Publishing Company
Post Mills, Vermont

Chelsea Green Publishing Company
PO Box 130, Route 113
Post Mills, VT 05058-0130

Judevine was designed and typeset in Bembo by Kate Mueller/Chelsea Green Publishing Company. It was printed on Glatfelter, an acid-free paper, by Thomson-Shore, Inc.

Library of Congress Cataloging-in-Publication Data

Budbill, David.
    Judevine : the complete poems, 1970–1990 / by David Budbill
        p. cm.
    Includes index.
    ISBN 0–930031–47–4. — ISBN 0–930031–48–2 (pbk.)
    I. Title.
    PS3552.U346J83   1991
    811'.54—dc20   91–23481
                                                         CIP

for Lois and Nadine

ACKNOWLEDGMENTS

Grateful acknowledgment to the following magazines in which some of these poems first appeared: *Arachne, The Beloit Poetry Journal, Bleb/ The Ark, Claymore, Common Sense, Country Journal, Format: Art and the World, The Great Circumpolar Bear Cult, The Greenfield Review, The Greensboro Review, Harvard Magazine, Jam-today, Longhouse, New Letters, North Coast Poetry, The Ocooch Mountain News, The Ohio Review, Organic Gardening and Farming, Poetry Now, Poets Who Sleep #10, Quest/79, The Road Apple Review, Rumors Dreams and Digressions, Seeds of Change, Tamarack, Truck, The Vermont Vanguard Press, The Vermont Peace Reader,* and *White Pine Journal.*

"Raymond and Ann" first appeared in *Harper's Magazine.*

"Why I Came to Judevine" first appeared in *The Ohio Review* under the title, "Man at the Breech: My Uncle Freddy."

Portions of this book were originally published as *The Chain Saw Dance* by The Crow's Mark Press in 1977 and subsequently by Countryman Press in 1983; and as *From Down to the Village* by The Ark in 1981; and as *Pulp Cutters' Nativity* by The Countryman Press in 1981; and as *Why I Came to Judevine* by White Pine Press in 1987.

The quotation from Thomas Merton in "Going Places" is taken from his essay "The Sacred City" as it appears in *Ishi Means Man,* published by Unicorn Press, Inc. in 1976, and is used here with permission of the publisher.

The original settler's narrative in "Journey for the North" is my adaptation of a memoir published by Seth Hubbell in the 1884 edition of *Child's Gazetteer of Orleans and Lamoille Counties, Vermont.*

Pulp Cutters' Nativity is my adaptation of *The Second Shepherds' Play,* an English miracle play written about 1450.

A note of thanks is due the many actors in theaters around the country who have played in my play *Judevine: The Play in Two Acts,* which is adapted from this collection. Through their enthusiastic portrayals of these characters and from their improvisations, I have gained much. I am grateful to them all.

CONTENTS

PART III

PART IV

And, wel I woot, as ye goon by the weye,
Ye shapen yow to talen and to playe;
For trewely confort ne myrthe is noon
To ride by the weye doumb as a stoon;
And therefore wol I maken yow disport,
As I seyde erst, and doon yow som confort. . . .

And, for to make yow the moore mury,
I wol myselven gladly with yow ride
Right at myn owene cost, and be youre gide.

Geoffrey Chaucer
The Canterbury Tales

PART I

HERMIE

Hermie Newcome lived in a bread truck on the edge
of Bear Swamp.
The bread truck is still there
with a spruce tree through the roof and the remains
of his last pig pen.
He had a bunk up front where the seats used to be
so in the morning he could wake up and look out
the windshield at the day.
There was a little wood stove in the back.
Hermie brought the stove wood in
through the rear doors so he wouldn't have to
lug it through his bedroom.
There was a table and a chair
and some crates for cupboards.
It was always neat in there.
It was a good place and cozy.
Hermie didn't need anything big as a bus.

His woman, Florence, was an Indian from New York.
Before he lived in the bread truck, they had a shack
next to the Dunn Hill cemetery and before that
they lived on Hermie's family place
on the Aiken Pond road up from the schoolhouse
where I used to live.
But one night while they were still at the home place,
Hermie got pissed at something, nobody knows what,
and flew into a rage, which he did about twice a week,
but this time went too far and lit both house and barn
and watched them burn.
When the neighbors came Hermie was out in the snow,
in the dooryard stomping and screaming:
Burn! Goddamnit!
Burn! you wuthless place.
You never was no goddamn good!

Nobody could ever be quite sure when Hermie was drunk.
He acted crazy all the time.
There's nothing left of the Newcome place now,
only the spring box. Those tamarack boards
will last forever.

Then they moved over to the shack by the cemetery.
Hermie liked it there,
said it was the first place he ever lived
where he had decent neighbors.

Antoine tells about going past there on a Saturday night
and seeing
Hermie and Florence dancing with the chain saw going
in the middle of the floor.
Hermie and Florence'd get drunk,
then Hermie would adjust the carburetor on the saw
so it would run too rich
so it would sputter, bounce with a rhythm
worthy of a good musician.
Then they'd sing and dance
to the music of the saw.

Hermie could cut pulp like a son of a bitch;
he could bull and jam when he wanted to,
but that wasn't very often.
Everybody said he was worthless.
Hiram still says
his mother should of knocked him in the head when he was born
and spent the money on some grain to raise a pig.

Hermie never did anybody any harm;
in fact the night he burnt the home place
he was sure to get Florence and the cats out
before he struck the match.

He burnt the cemetery place too.
That's when Florence left him, went back
to the reservation or to Morrisville.
I don't know where.

Then he moved alone into the bread truck in the swamp.
Hermie spent his life looking for the perfect place.
That's what all those fires were about.
And in the end he found that place.
The bread truck wouldn't burn.

OLD MAN PIKE

Old man Pike was a sawyer at the mill
in Craftsbury.
He lived just down the road from here.
Every morning he walked six miles through the woods
over Dunn Hill saddle while the sun rose.
He took dinner and supper in the village,
then walked home across the mountain in the dark.
Sally Tatro who used to live on my place
would hear him coming through the night, singing.
Sometimes he'd stop to gossip
but mostly she only saw him stride by the window
and disappear.

The old man could have stayed at home,
milked cows, like everybody else,
but he needed an excuse to go and come
through the mountains, every day,
all his life, alone.

Old man Pike didn't believe in the local religion of work,
but out of deference, to his neighbors maybe,

he bowed to it,
placed its dullness at the center of his life,
but he was always sure, because of his excuse,
to wrap it at the edges of his days
in the dark and solitary amblings of his pleasure.

ANSON

Anson was born on the place next door, half a mile away.

About ten years ago the university took part of the Boynton place
    for taxes.
(The university, by the way, has been delinquent on the taxes ever
    since.)
Not long after that the Boyntons sold out, but Anson came back a
    few years ago
with a French wife and two sons to farm his home.
He rented from the owner, a chiropractor in California.
Anson sold out last spring.
The bank wouldn't loan him money for machinery
because he didn't own the place and because
the chiropractor wouldn't give him a long-term lease.

Anson's gone.
Kicked off the place he was born on
by somebody he never met.

They were good neighbors. My boy and their boys
played together, rode their bikes up and down the road,
built forts in the woods, fished for trout in the brook,
gave each other courage to make it through a day at school.

Anson spread shit on our garden free of charge,
helped me draw my wood, used to take all three boys

on a sleigh behind his snow machine.
Marie took the boys to Morrisville to the movies.
She was pretty and alive. It was fun
to watch her move across a room.
We never visited all that much but they were good neighbors.

Anson busted his ass over there. It was his home
even if he did have to rent it. He busted his ass
and for nothing.

Everybody says the Boynton place is jinxed,
says nobody can make a go of it over there.
Anson could have if he'd had a break.
It's not the farm that's jinxed; it's farming.
Grain goes up, milk goes down.
The U.S. secretary of agriculture has deliberately
conspired against the family farm.
The name of the game in Washington is agribusiness,
huge consolidated farms big as Continental Can.
Down there they want the family farm to die.
They want fewer and fewer people
to have more and more money.

This is not my fantasy.
The Associated Press reported last week
that the secretary of agriculture admitted during a senate hearing
that he thought the family farm should be "phased out."

Here's the secretary again: "Farming isn't a way of life.
It's a way to make a living."
God forbid somebody should see his life and living
as the same thing. What are these idiot neighbors of mine
doing anyway thinking they should love their work?
Don't they know the end of work is money?

Listen, this isn't an issue doesn't concern you.

7

This issue is the death knell
for what little anarchistic independence is left.
It is oligarchy's fanfare,
and the band plays louder every day.

Every summer Anson had a window box of flowers
near the milk house door
and every morning after chores
he watered them and then
with the thumb and forefinger of his calloused hand
he gently, gently plucked
the dying blossoms.

As I was saying, last May, on a Saturday, Anson and Marie
sold out. It was a good day.
Anson's prayers were answered.
He'd asked God not to let it rain.
As the sun came up Norman Pelletier—
the auctioneer—
drove down Route 15 and up over the hill
to here and told Marie
to have an hour's worth of junk
to get the people started.

By ten o'clock trucks lined both sides the road
either way from their house half a mile to ours
and that far the other way too.
It was a farmer's auction, too early in the year
for summer people hunting antiques.
There weren't any antiques anyway.
Marie moved around the crowd forcing a smile and waving
like a maître d' serving up her life.

There was soda and hot dogs
and kids running around screaming, excited by the crowd.
Edith cried. So did Marie. Anson wanted to but didn't.

The farmers stood around and bid, raising a hand quietly,
nodding a head.
But there weren't any jokes.
They knew they were playing bit parts in a movie
about their own deaths.

At the end of the day
Anson had taken in thirty-seven thousand dollars
and all that in just machinery and stock.
Everybody said he done real good, *real* good.
But it wasn't good enough.

Anson's working as a mechanic in Burlington now.
He makes a hundred ten dollars a week for his family of four.
They've got a trailer in a trailer park.
We saw them a couple of months ago.
They said they missed it up here on the hill.

BILL

The Pikes have come a long way down
since the old man walked to Craftsbury
every day all his life to saw boards.
There's only Bill and Arnie left as far as I know
and both of them make only enough to stay drunk.

About five years ago one night in January
I dug Bill out of a snowbank.
It was two in the morning and thirty below.
He'd driven off the road where it crosses Bear Swamp.
He was dead drunk.
In fact, when I waded through the snow to his car
I thought he *was* dead,
and he would have been by morning,

of cold or carbon monoxide,
if I or someone hadn't come along.
The headlights were on and the radio, and Bill
slumped across the wheel with the motor running.
I banged on the door, opened it,
Bill rolled out, head first, into the snow, like a corpse.
I drug him to my car.
As the snow on his face melted, he woke up a little.
Probably he'd been to Cole's Pond Bottle Club.
It was Saturday night.

I shook him, asked him where he wanted to go.
All he did was point toward the village.
I knew when we got to Judevine he'd point to Hardwick,
then Danville, Newport, Derby, Eden,
on and on like that for days
while I drove around the ass end of the state and he sobered up,
which would be some time since
he brought the Bud with him.
But the bastard pointed me to Arnie's place
without the slightest error.

I think blind drunks have homing devices, like the ones in geese,
pickled in their livers.
They don't need to see, only point.
They know where home is.

Arnie was still up, drunk too.
I got him to come out and the two of us drug Bill up
over the rotten porch steps
and into a garbage can of empties.
We made such a racket getting him across the porch and into the
    house that the blue tick out back started howling.
We dumped him on the living room linoleum and I left.
Nobody said thank-you or good-bye.
In fact, in the years since nobody has ever mentioned the incident,

except once down at the garage Bill said "'lo" to me
and in his eyes there was the look of recognition.

We bought a pig from Bill one spring.
When I went into his rusty trailer to pay him
the place smelled like baby shit and kerosene.

The railroad's started up again
and Bill's got his old job back
when he's sober.
He still raises pigs I guess although I don't know
since even though his place is only a few miles from here
I haven't been past there in years.

I still see him now and then working on the tracks
or buying beer at the garage
but we never speak.

We don't know each other.

ANTOINE

Spring.
My first day as a laborer on a Christmas tree farm.
I pulled my pickup to the side of the road,
hopped over a drainage ditch running full
and started up a slope toward a man
standing about a quarter mile away.
Even now, the first of May,
the woods still stood in better than a foot of rotten snow,
but here where the earth tilted south the ground was bare.
Above the grays and browns of last year's matted grass
the young Christmas trees seemed iridescent
in the morning sun.

Antoine stood motionless, watching me come up the hill.

You da new mans? Taut you was. Mike said you
was caumin'. I'm Antoine LaMotte! I live alone
ina trailer up on Aiken Pond. Shitagoddamn!
good to be in da sun again!

He offered me a cigarette and lit us both.

Antoine is a small man, five two or three.
About his cheeks there is that unmistakable alcoholic sheen.
His neck moves in deepening shades of red toward the back until
between his hair line and his collar
it is the color of wild strawberries.
His hair is thin but black and his dark eyes dance
when he talks, which he does incessantly.
His whole body moves with the rhythm of his words;
his hands flutter in front of him as if they were
dancing to the music of his speech.
He walks like a duck.
He bangs around the house of his body like a baby.
He is small, feather light, delicate and infinitely tender.

We stood for a long time smoking, looking out
over the mountains.

Wall! you mus' be crazy fauckin' basterd take
a job like dis! Bull an' jam like da rest of us
for two an' a korter an'our. You crazy as me!
By Chris' an' Saint Teresa don't you say I didn't
warn you. Before you're done, your tongue hang out,
touchhole hang daown, you pull an' tug 'till
you cast your wid'ers. Your mamma
roll over in 'er grave, cry out,
Oh! by Jesus, how I fail you as a mudder!
When you go home tonight your little wimens

12

she gonna haf 'ta take a rain check.
She gonna hate you tonight!
An' you gonna start to hate dese friggin' trees.
You gonna wish your mudder be a baby girl!

Wall, what else is dere ta do? No goddamn work
'raound here anymore. Guess you know dat
else you weren't be daum enough to be 'ere.
Naow! no work. No work atall.
Can't mi'k caows anymore.
I yanked does titties, shauveled dat shit, all my life, den
dey caum an' say I gots to haf' a bulk tank,
an' I can't keep a pig in da barn, an' I godda wash
my han's in dis and my feets in dat, julluk I be
some kinda brain sergen or sut'in.'
So I say shit to dat an' haf a nauction
an' I be glad to git done too, fer 'bout a day.
Den I begin dreamin' 'bout dem caows and haf' a version.
I could see 'em standin' in der stalls. My little
girlfriends, an' I wander 'raound dat empty barn
an' oh! by Jesus, I was sick in my heart!
Nat'in' to do wi' my days. Naut'in'.
So I caum crawlin' over here, work out,
be saumbody else's slave, 'steada my own,
an' now I sleep in one of dem friggin' ice boxes
all to myself an' watch saum downcountry saumbody
tear daown my house an' barn what I was born in, shit!
Nat'in' ta do 'raound here nomore.

All da quarries over to Buffalo Mountain gone.
Stun sheds in Hardwick all fallin' daown.
Nat'in' over dere but rats and crazy ol' Artie Mezey
hidin' in da sheds inside an ol' car drinkin'
blackberry brandy an' waitin' for saum little boys
to caum along. Chris'! da whole goddamn taown
just fallin' in da reever. Ah! when I was a boy

it weren't dat way. Dey was mills an' bars.
T'irty-tew bars in dat little place!
Haf' good times der too, wall I guess!
Good whorehouse too. I used to go confession
over to da church on Friday afternoon
den step across da street take in a little matinee.
Da church still der, but da whorehouse she ain't.

When da sheds close daown dat town shrivel
like a moldy squash. Nat'in' left.
On'y saum ol' wop cudders, ones still livin',
what can't go out winners 'cause a da air, stayin' ta home
coughin' out der lungs. Ah! wadda you care!

There was an embarrassed silence.
Then he went on.

Wall, here we be, ain't we? No more sittin'
by da stof 'til Doc say you be done.
Shitagoddamn, goddamnashit, dis da right place to be
caum spring, bull an' jam 'raound here outin da sun
t'in yer blood. Don't need no tonic here, shitacat'sass naow!
Ol' Doc give us a tonic. Couple weeks a walkin'
twenty miles a day spredin' dis fauckin' fert'lizer
an' your blood'll be runnin' good. Rock. Jus' rock
ya know. Dat's what we're spreddin' all day long;
15-10-10 an' wha's da odder sistyfife? Rock!
'nert 'greedients is what dey try to tell you,
but don't you belieft, Mister Man, it's rock,
peacestone, from da mine, groun' up fine. Geewiss,
Geewiss Christ! ya'd t'ink a man a forty-five do saumt'in' sides
sprinkle rock onto baby trees. Hell, comeon.
I'llgetjabucket.

We set off down the hill toward a tractor and a wagon
piled with eighty-pound bags of Old Fox fertilizer.

14

What you really do, David? Dat's your name, ain't it? David?
I know somebody like the likes a you ain't gonna spend his en-tire
life makin' love to dese friggin' trees!
What's really why you be here on dis eart'?

I was afraid you'd ask.

Dat bad, eh?

Yes.

Wall, you can go ahead an' tell me, 'cause I known plenty
    criminal in my day,
an' I know how to keep my moud broken-down
an' ou'da order when I haf' to. Some day when we got more time
an' less money, I'll tell you what it be like araound dese parts
back in da Prohibition days! Den you see how not much
you could be could be so bad compared to den!
What you really do?

I'm a . . . writer. I'm . . . a poet.

What's dat you say?

I am a poet. I write poetry.

Shitacat'sass naow! You do? You be?
Oh, goddamnit to shit, I am a proud man to meet you!
Oh, my mudder in heaven look down on me!
I be workin' wid a poet! A *man* what writes poetry!
Fuck me! Next what we gonna see araound dese parts!
Ah, David, we gonna haf' a good time togedder!

An' don't you worry none. Your secret safe wid me!
Why, when I was a boy back in dat Prohibition day
dere was diamond ring bury in da dirt beneat' da porch

15

and submachine gun under da hay in da barn,
an' I never knew a t'ing about dem.
Ah, goddamnit to shit, I like poetry!

When I first knew Antoine he drank a lot,
a six-pack for breakfast on the way to work,
then another couple during the day.
I'm sure he drank himself to sleep.
But he never missed work and he never drank anything
but beer. He swore that if you drank only beer
you'd never become an alcoholic.

I'm no alacholic. Not like Uncle Clyde. He got
alacholic tumor big as a cabbage in his stomach.
Got to feed it brandy every day.
Me, I ain't nat'in' but a goddamn drunk.
Alacholism for da multitude millionaire. Politicians.
Poor fauckin' basterds da likes a me jus' goddamn drunks.

David, you like politics? I watch dat news
'baout ever' night. Watch dem crazy basterds
jomp araound. Goddamn multitude millionaires.
Gangsters. Any of 'em wort a turd get a bullet
in da head. All dem Kennedys and dat Martin
Lutter King. Oh Jesus! how I love dat man!
He like me, radder be a lover dan a fi'der.
See how far it got 'im! Naow! white man da biggest basterd
whatever live. Steal da country from da Indian
den make da nigger do da work!

Like me, da white nigger of da nord.

Wall, people's mean
all over. Up here it's skinhead 'gainst da frog.
I know what dey call me an' I don' care.
Let 'em call me what dey want if dat's da way

16

dey get der pleasure. Elwin tol' me what Alfreda said
'baout me not havin' no more brains 'an a frog's got feadders.
Wall, she got peacesoup in her veins too! Hell, wadda I care.
Nigger a da nord, dat's me, an' I don' care.
Poof! I know plenty. I just can' t'ink of it.
I see frogs she never wid hands big as hams,
once I even seen a snake wid legs up on Stannard Mountain,
but shit if I ever see a frog wid feadders.
Jus' 'cause she marry a skinhead drunk she t'ink herself
better 'an her gra'ma. She eat dem legs too.
Hell to her! You get yourself a bran sack full, skin 'em easy,
roll 'em flour, salt, pepper, fry 'em quick,
haf' a couple beers and, by Jesus, Mister, you got sut'in' good.

Then Antoine met Shirley.
They lived together in a trailer
up in Collinsville with her two boys.
About a month after all of us knew what was going on,
Antoine finally said:

David! got me a wimens! Workin' out, too. Workin' out good.
Two-hunnert-t'irty poun' and not an ounce a fat.
Caum up here from Joisey. Dat's how she say it.
Dat's how she talk.

She say, Hoi, Antoine, moi name's Shoiley. Oi just moved up heah
from New Joisey.
Would you boi any chance happen to have a glass
of wudder? Shitacat'sass, ain't dat funny?
Ah! it make me laugh da way she talk.

She is a good wimens.
I'd marry her tomorrow if it weren't we loose da welfare,
an' her wid dem two outlaw boys.
My rockin' chair money ain't enauf. Was for me,
get me tru da winner, but ain't for four a us.

If we be only two, be okay, but she got dem bad actin' saverges.
Shitagoddamn, if we be only two . . .
Wall, better'n livin' to myself in dat trailer
wi' nathin' but my goddamn dog.

It lasted about a year.
Then Shirley left, went down to a place in Barre.

David, she lef' me. Walk right aout. Poof!
I back in dat trailer wi' dat friggin' dog.
Only frien' I got. Two friggin' dogs.
Alone again. Just like dat goddamn Hermie.
Ah! goddamnit to shit, what's da use!
Piss on dat fire. Let's go drink saum beer.
Comeon, David, drink beer wid me.
Let's go drink saum beer.

I didn't go and I've been sorry ever since.
Antoine began missing more and more work until he was
    showing up about once a week.
That's when Bert fired him.

About a month after Antoine got fired he came over to my place
one Saturday afternoon. He was filthy. His eyes were beets.
He hadn't shaved in weeks.
He had a quart of Schaefer in his hand.

Dawyd, how yew be? Ah ain't tu good. Fawk,
Ah'm 'cinegratin', Dawyd. Caumin' apart tew pieces.
Ah doan know what Ah'm gonna dew. Ah didn't know ah luf
dat wimens so. Ah didn't know it. Mah mamma she be right.
Ah Christ, Ah wish to hell she still be a baby girl.

I didn't see Antoine for another couple months.
Then, again on a Saturday afternoon, he showed up,
clean clothes and shaven. He looked like his old self,

only better.

David! shitacat'sass, we back togedder!
Naow you better sid daown.
Dis gonna get you in da stomach,
right between da shoulder blades.

David, I gonna be a fadder!
By Christ, I never taut it caum to be.
Oh, my mamma be so pleased. She die t'inkin'
she fails me as a mudder, t'ink I gonna end my days
a smelly bach'er drunk. Dah last time midnight
New Year's Eve I caum in kneel at my fadder,
da year he die, I be turdy den, an get da blessin'
when he puts his han' on my head an' say da words
I know he a'mos' cry 'cause he know he iss dyin' and he know
I spen' my days yankin' my tool an' spillin' my seed.

Now dat little wimens got me growin' in 'er an',
Oh by Jesus, I be happy as a puppy to da road!
Oh! I wish to hell I could marry her!
She caum home from docter, sit daown a' table,
tell me, we bod' cry all afternoon, be so happy.
Next day I go to docter's say you help me naow,
I can' be drunk no more, I'm gonna be a fadder.
He say I be alacholic, I say Naow! how dat be!
I taut nobody be alacholic what drink only beer.
Dat's why I never drink dat hard stuff. He say, You are.
I didn't know it! Shitagoddamn, all dah years me t'ink
I nat'in' but a goddamn drunk I be high class alacholic
julluk da president!

He say I quit or I never see my baby grow,
and by Jesus dat t'ree week ago an' I ain't pull a ring since.
An' I ain't gonna to needer. We gonna name 'im . . . Pierre.
And if he be a girl, Michelle. Shitagoddamn, David,

naow I be like you book writers, I got my head
in da cloud, no more on da graoun' dan da moon,
an' Doc gimme my job back too. I tol' 'im
I got my reason to work naow. Fauck me!
I'll pick bluebird shit off da White Cliffs of Dover
if I haf' to.

Shirley had the baby and Antoine stomped around
like a bandy rooster.
Then it was spring again.

Graoun's a bullin', David. Time to plant da seed.
You got to make your wedder. Got to do it naow.
Just da right time. It's mudder nature. Like a wimens.
You be like me last year, cabbage an' tomato
gone to hell but I get a sidehill a patada
an' a baby girl. Dis year Poppa gonna plow
da whole goddamn state for his gardin!

Oh Jesus, I a'mos' forgot, dat hippie girl live up da road
caum over see da baby. She lean over coo,
her titties hangin' daown loose so big
dey weren't fid a sap bugit,
an' I see her pussy too stickin' out her pants
big as a witches broom. Bah gosh, David! how I wish
I be dat little baby!
Hell, an ol' buck got a stiff horn an' I ain't be done yet!

Shit, David, we got to get unmarried from dese goddamn trees!
I'm sick of it! I'm goin' home. Two o'clock an' I don't care.
I'm goin' to da matinee. I be!
I got to see dat wimens and my little baby.

You tell Doc I ain't functionatin' right today.
Tell 'im . . . I be back tamarra!

ARNIE

Arnie and I harvested Christmas trees three falls together.
Arnie is emaciated and always dirty.
He shaves only on Saturday nights
before he goes to the bottle club.
His face is more wretched than any I have ever seen.
All I remember about those falls together
is how much Arnie knew about the Second World War
and how his nose dripped.
He'd stand in the snow and shiver like a popple leaf
and his nose would drip.
He never bothered to wipe it
except maybe two or three times a day
he'd sop it gently
with the back of the glove on his right hand.
He had a filthy, ragged, black-and-green Johnson Woolen Mills
    jacket he wore summer and winter.
He stole it from the Mount Mansfield Company
when he worked there on the lifts, which is okay with me
since those in Stowe steal more from the likes of Arnie
than the likes of Arnie could ever imagine stealing from them.

Don't get me wrong. Arnie's no saint.
No proletarian archetype.
He's always in court.
He's a bad actor and everybody knows it.
But if we're going to discuss gangsters,
let's talk about the big time.

About Stowe, ski capital of the East, Stowe:
stolen from and supported by the state of Vermont.
The beautiful people's island plunked down
in the middle of the filth and loneliness
that stretches from Maine to Georgia, from top to bottom,
all the way down the Appalachian chain.

Let's talk about the thousands of farms gone under
so nice folks, like you, can have a place to lie around.
About a state of native slaves hanging around all winter
living off unemployment and welfare
waiting for the summer rich so they can mow a lawn
or paint a house for two and a quarter an hour.

Let's talk about the Vermont Development Department
and the "Beckoning Country," about their photographs
in *The New York Times* of white houses, red barns,
dirt roads and pretty cows, about why they don't take pictures
of Arnie's house or East Judevine or Hardwick or Island Pond
or a hundred other wretched towns. About why they don't
take pictures of kids with body lice or pictures of old ladies
who freeze to death in their beds. Let's talk about why
the legislators let their neighbors rot while they suck up
to those with money from Boston and New York, about how
four times a year *Vermont Life* sells a slick, full-color tumble
down the dreamy pit of nostalgia where,
for just two dollars a throw, you can sit wreathed
in an imaginary past.

Let's talk about the guy from Greenwich, Connecticut
with five thousand dollars worth of skis on his car
going down the road past Arnie Pike who makes
five thousand dollars a year.

I remember one day—in the fall, I think. It was warm
and we'd eaten lunch and were lying around with our boots off
talking about everything and laughing
and somehow I said—because I am who I am:
Life's really good, most of the time.
Something like that anyway.
And Arnie began shaking his head slowly and his eyes
got sad and: Naw, he said,
Naw. Not fer me.

Most athe time it ain't.
Then Arnie raised his head quick,
or as quick as slow Arnie could,
and his face had been transformed.
It was ghoulish, terrifying, as if the gates of hell
had tried to swallow him and he had got away.
Then he bared his rotten teeth and said, slow,
with a grin, while his nose dripped:
But ah'll survive.

Arnie and the other East Judevine uglies will survive,
in spite of the Mountain Company. They will survive
hidden away from downcountry skiers and the big money.
They will survive, wretchedly, but they will survive.
And when everybody thinks the gene pool has withered
to a ski bum and his après-ski bunny, then,
unknown to everyone who's supposed to know,
the ways of staying alive will still be known
by a few outlaws living in shacks
along the banks of the Wild Branch.

I was at Arnie's place just once after I took Bill there that night.
It was only a week before Arnie burnt out.
He always said he never bothered with fuses.
Pennies was just as good and cheaper.
Then he'd laugh and show his ugly teeth.
His place smelled like kerosene.
Nobody ever did know exactly why he burnt out,
but Arnie's no Hermie Newcome. He's too timid.
He didn't light it.
It was either the pot burner or the pennies.
Arnie survived.

It was the time I'm talking about when I was there
drinking beer at Arnie's place that he told me, and this
after knowing him five years, that he always had a doe

down cellar—always—year round:
I don't care nathin' fer the warden. He's afraid
ta caum up here. When Sam Raymond was around
he'd turn away.
Hell, he was an outlaw hisself.
That's why they made 'im warden.

Arnie went down to Massachusetts for a couple of years
to work in a shoe factory.
I guess he made pretty good money,
but he couldn't stand it down there.

One fall we were cutting trees up on Elmore Mountain
when color was still in the hills.
It was a clear day and we were up toward the top of the lot
looking out over the Lamoille valley at Eden Mountain
about thirty miles away.
That's when Arnie, Arnie the Wretched, the Ugly, the Stupid,
the Drunk, the Outlaw, the Poor—
that's when Arnie said:

Lookit 'at. 'At's why I live here.

And we looked across the ancient green and brown
and red and yellow mountains and the sky was blue
and some fleecy clouds and an osprey hunted the Lamoille
and we stood there while Arnie's nose dripped
and listened to the wind slip through the spruce trees.

✦ ✦ ✦

ANTOINE AND I GO FISHING

Saints an' me! I quit!

Look at what we live wid: Bert
an' he sayin' someday he iss gonna catch me workin'
when he come out here in da puckerbrush in his bat'room slipper
an' peek araoun' to spy on us. Wall, someday he might be,
but, by Jesus Christ, David, let's don't let it be today!

You know—you pro'bly don't—we been workin'
in dis lot all summer and up dis loggin' road
less'n half a mile is a pond what's full of trout,
I mean, Mister, full. I been t'inkin' on it all dis summer
an' today's da day we go up dere an' get our supper.

Poachin' and jackin' ain't too much for me;
I don't go sugarin' da way ol' Elwin use' to
wid a tank in back da trunk and gadder after dark
roadside buckets offin saumbody else's trees.
Dat's narrow.
Makin' sugar is too much work for dat!

But dese trout here naow just up da hill
is a differ'nt matter entirely since all Doc done
was drop a few into dat place when he built da t'ing.
Da fishes did da rest. So da way I see it
dey ain't no more his 'an anybody else's since da ones
he bought be caught or died long time ago,
an' what's left is only fishes what belong each odder
or demselves or to dem what hooks 'em
like da likes a you an' me.

Now how dat be? You t'ink I cipher good enough
get us up dere?

Oh, you don't have to worry none 'bout him caumin'.
I know Doc, know 'im well; he'd shoot us
just like he do his gramma. Nice fella, him.

Comeon, David, I bring you pole, put two in da trunk
dis mornin'. You scratch araound, get some worm,
I get da 'quip'ment an' we go.

I did as I was told and we were gone
up the hill into the shade of trees
and to the pond. In fifteen minutes
we had half a dozen of the nicest brook trout
I have ever seen.

Then Antoine startled:
Ho! Hear dat! Come on!
It's him, or Bert.
One shoot, d'odder fire.

Six trout flapping from an alder stick.
Two men run and stumble, giggle,
through the woods
back to the car.

Antoine hid the poles and fish inside his trunk
and we listened to a log truck
grinding down the hill toward the village:

Wall, six be da poacher's limit anyway.

WHY I CAME TO JUDEVINE

I

Cleveland. 1953.

Gertrude and Freddy, my aunt and uncle, live on the East Side,
  Alhambra Street, an Italian neighborhood.

Freddy's last name was Modine.

He ran a metal lathe at Picker X-Ray.

A good job; he didn't have to go outside and therefore had work
  in any weather, and he didn't have to lift or bend,

and the union scale was good or better than anything he had ever
  known before.

Alhambra Street was trying hard in 1953 to raise itself above its
  past.

Everyone washed and waxed his car at least once a week,

kept a postage stamp lawn of creeping bent, smoother, greener,
  more dense than any golf green in existence.

And Alhambra Street was trying hard to do away with street life.

Standing and drinking in the open was not a part of its vision of
  the future. People stayed inside, to themselves,

watched their new TV's, just like the people in the suburbs.

Going there may have been impossible, but acting like it was not.

But on summer evenings the old ways came back.

Maybe it was just the city heat, no breeze, or maybe it was
  remorse for such total abjuration of the past.

Whatever it was, it drew them out onto the porches.

Two porches to every house, one up, one down, what we called a
  "double house"—a house on top of a house.

Because of the climb the upper house was rented cheaper, but on
  summer nights, when the porches filled,

it was the better place to be.

You could lean on the railing and command the street.

On those summer evenings the men came home from the
    factories in their shiny Fords and Chevys,
squeezed them into narrow drives between the houses, climbed
    the stairs, drank their beer, ate their garlic and sausages,
then left the television dark and went onto the porches.

They sat on gliders, smoked and rocked;
or put themselves backward into straight-backed chairs, folded
    their arms over the tops,
and stared blankly into the street.
Then, slowly, the shouting from porch to porch, back and forth,
    began,
about how if that nigger Larry Doby struck out one more time
    they'd kill the bastard.
And in their hearts they were angry, jealous, and resentful that a
    black man, so handsome, smooth, and famous,
could be the subject of their voices.

Then the women, the fat women, having done the dishes, also
    came onto the porches
and sat on the gliders and also rocked, their hands folded gently
    across their abdomens,
laid gently like little balls of dough on their damp aprons.
Or they stood, the outside heel of each wrist propped on their
    hips, fingers dangling.

After the women settled themselves, the men would rise,
as if unnerved by the presence of their wives,
lean over the railing and stare, or pace a bit across the porch
in their white socks, their ubiquitous undershirts—
not T-shirts, those were for another class, another age,
but undershirts—sleeveless, white and ribbed,
and their beer bellies drooping.

They were factory workers, all of them, every one, employees of
American Steel, Republic Steel, Jones and Laughlin,

Hanna Paints, Glidden Paints, Addressograph-Multigraph,
Van Dorn Iron, U.S. Aluminum, Picker X-Ray,
Allied Chemical, Apex Motors, White Motors,
Cleveland Hardware, Clark Controller, Cleveland Welding,
Ferro Manufacturing, Eberhard Manufacturing,
Eton Manufacturing, Chase Brass, Cleveland Graphite,
Vulcan Tool and Die, Tinnerman Speednut,
American Spool and Wire;
house after double house, street after street,
Italians, Lithuanians, Slavs, Poles, Hungarians, Slovaks,
neighborhood pressed against neighborhood,
and union men every one,
United Steel Workers of America,
United Chemical Workers of America,
United Sheet Metal Workers of America,
UAW, UEW,
AFL and CIO,
every one.

When the evening began to darken and they felt the cool air on
    their naked arms,
the people went inside and turned on their televisions.
But when my Uncle Freddy left the porch, he passed through the
    living room into the kitchen where, maybe,
he took down from the cupboard a new pack of Camels,
then moved slowly, almost shuffling, to the hallway,
the bathroom in front of him, the bedroom to his right, and to
    his left, the spare bedroom, his den.

Maybe he paused there in the hallway for a moment, and slowly
    opened the new pack of cigarettes, slowly lit one,
wheezed his emphysemic wheeze a time or two,
and waited to smell the heavy tobacco smoke mix with the
    smells of supper's tomato sauce and pasta.
Then he turned toward the door of his den
and closed himself inside that room for the evening.

29

I was only in his den a couple of times;
once would have been enough.
Forty years later that place is as vivid to me as the mountains are
outside my window at this moment.

II

Stand in the doorway. Step in.
Turn right and face the outside wall.
There is one window in the middle with a dark green shade,
the kind for keeping out all light, perhaps left over from the
blackouts during the war. The shade is always drawn.
Old and dirty, green and silver wallpaper is on the wall, as on all
the walls in this room.
To the right of the window, a calendar with a photograph of a
mostly naked woman.
Her lips are pursed. She stares outward, a catatonic stare,
the kind Kim Novak stared at William Holden from the swing in
the park in the motion picture *Picnic.*

Turn left and face another wall. There is a day-bed up against this
one; it is also green but darker than the walls.
Next to it, to the left, a little wooden keg, and on top of it is a
stack of worn copies of *Saga* and *Field & Stream.*
Uncle Freddy never read anything but *Saga* and *Field & Stream*—
he never read the newspaper.

Tacked to the wall above the couch is a fake leopard skin, cut from
some car upholstery, and hooked to it,
dangling treacherously, are a dozen fishing lures:
musky baits, big ones,
some of them a foot long, looking ludicrous and mean.
They hang there waiting for water, action,
a monstrous fish gored through the mouth,
thrashing and boiling the lake behind the boat,
a man, my Uncle Freddy, at the other end of the line, his teeth
clenched in battle,

his lips slightly smiling, his blood banging against his temples.

And above the leopard skin and baits, also fastened to the wall, are
two fishing rods and reels, crossed like swords.

Turn left again and face another wall.
High up in the right-hand corner, where the ceiling and the walls
converge, a minnow seine
drapes gracefully halfway to the center of the ceiling,
filling the corner and sagging almost halfway to the floor.
The soft curves of the brown netting make a hammock, and in the
hammock
a few pieces of water-worn cork and a piece of gray, feather light
driftwood rest gently, in a stillness they must have known
once on a summer evening, the sun going down, water lapping
against the shore.

In the center of this wall stands Uncle Freddy's gun cabinet.
Once, maybe twice, Uncle Freddy had unlocked the glass door
and let me hold the guns.
There was a .218 Bee with an 8-power Weaver scope for killing
woodchucks,
and a big 12-gauge Ithaca with a 30-inch barrel and full choke for
ducks and geese,
and a Winchester 94, a .30-30, for deer.
But the object of my desire, the only one I cared about, was the
16-gauge, double-barrel, side-by-side, Fox.
The stock and forearm were delicately checkered,
and the dark walnut glistened with a deep patina from years of
Freddy's oil and rubbing.
At the breech, engraved in the metal, was a tiny hunting scene of
a man and a dog at point and a partridge exploding away and
trees and grass, and all that
in a space no more than two inches long by one inch high.
It was a vision of our dream.

I always hoped when Freddy died I'd get that 16-gauge, but I didn't. I didn't even get it after Aunt Gertrude died.

All the guns were immaculately clean. They looked new, and the truth is, they were; none had ever been fired.

Freddy kept the shells and cartridges in a small drawer at the bottom of the gun cabinet.
There was one box of shells for each gun, four boxes, four different kinds of shells. And each box was full,
but the boxes were tattered and worn from years of having the cartridges taken out and handled and put back again.

III

Freddy and I went hunting together only once.
It was a Saturday, and we drove an hour and a half to Joe Paluchek's place in Ashtabula.
Paluchek worked at the plant with Uncle Freddy, but he had moved away from the East Side, had gotten out,
had bought ten acres in the country, or what went for country on the edges of Cleveland.
Paluchek was the envy of his friends. He had a crummy house on a crummy ten acres, but it was land and it was his.
I'd heard about him for years. He was the guy who could piss off his back porch and go hunting in his own back yard.
An hour and a half drive from home to work, one way, was not too much to pay, and everybody knew it.

Joe came out to greet us. He was standing very straight and his chest, it seemed to me, was puffed out.
He took Uncle Freddy by the hand, slapped him on the back and said: Welcome to the country!
And Uncle Freddy looked around and said, all the way into the kitchen: You sure got a nice place here, Joe.
And Joe said: Well, it ain't much, but it's mine and it's home and I can piss off my back porch and hunt in my own back yard.

And Freddy smiled and shook his head.

We sat at the kitchen table and had coffee and doughnuts and the
    two men talked and I listened.
They did not talk about the union or the plant.
They talked about hunting and game and their guns and about
    a fishing trip they thought they should take next summer.
Finally Joe thought it was time to get going, so we put on our
    hunting clothes;
the two men loaded their shotguns—I didn't have a gun—and we
    struck off into the field behind the house.

It was a hot November day and dusty.
After what seemed like a very short time, Joe kicked up a
    cottontail and killed it, almost blowing it in half.
Joe said it was a good sign, that the game was on the move today,
but we thrashed through that little field the rest of the morning
    and never saw another living thing.

Joe's property line at the back was a chain-link fence,
    and beyond the fence there was a graveyard of sorts for old
    tractor-trailer rigs,
a couple of acres probably, paved over with cement that was now
    heaved and cracked with age,
where dozens of old tractors and trailers stood, rusting and dented,
    with flat tires or no tires at all and broken windshields
and some broken beer bottles, and all this was silent and still,
except maybe in a slight breeze the back door to one of the trailer
    rigs would creak slightly on its rusting hinges.

I stood for a long time, the others having gone on, with my
    fingers hooked into the fence and stared
at the place beyond, the clutter and rubble. I turned away
and moved through the grimy little field toward the men.

IV

It was almost dark when we got back to Alhambra Street.
Joe had given us the rabbit, and we had laid it out gently on some
    newspaper in the trunk.
By the time Uncle Freddy had parked the car in the driveway and
    opened the trunk, a half dozen neighbors
were standing around waiting to see what we had to show.
Everyone was strangely quiet
as they stared down on the blood-soaked fur of the cottontail.

A rabbit, a wild rabbit, here, on Alhambra Street, in Cleveland,
    Ohio,
an animal that just this morning had lived in a field, slept under a
    bush, drunk from a brook,
an animal that lived far away, in the country, in Ashtabula.
For a moment these workers in factories had been drawn away
into a common past, to a time when they were all hunters, all
close to the country, and their reverential silence was for that time
    long ago
and for the sense of loss they all felt at being who and where they
    were now.

We gutted and skinned the rabbit, took it upstairs to the kitchen,
    quartered it, put it to soak, and went into the den,
where we cleaned the gun, even though it had not been fired,
and put it back in the gun cabinet and locked the door.

V

Turn left again and face the fourth and final wall.
On the right is the door.
Attached to the rest of the wall is a long workbench
with a grindstone and a vise bolted to it and resting on it an
    ashtray, two hunting knives and some fishing tackle.
There is a swivel chair on casters, the kind secretaries use or
    people who do delicate piecework on assembly lines.

Above the workbench is the focus of the entire room.
A painting, a reproduction of an oil, big, four foot by two, on
    cardboard with those squiggly lines to make it look like brush
    strokes,
of the Rockies, maybe the Tetons, with half their height above
    tree line and snow on the top, even now in early fall,
and in the foreground
a mountain meadow with flowers, asters maybe, blue anyway,
and in the middle ground a glacial lake, a reflecting mirror for the
    mountains,
and on the lake, resting like a dragonfly or an aspen leaf,
a canoe with a man in it fishing, alone, alone
in this vast and pristine wilderness.

There are two spotlights attached to the ceiling that shine down
    on the painting
so that Uncle Freddy can sit in the swivel chair in the dark,
and be lost.

I can see him, my Uncle Freddy,
sitting in his swivel chair, in the dark,
spotlights on the picture, his rifle or shotgun in his hands.
I can see him turn in the chair, quickly, snap the gun to his
    shoulder, and:
Pow! He says: Pow!

Again and again, night after night, year after year,
I see him turning in his chair. Or fishing on that lake,
his fly line unfurling, slowly, as in a dream, gracefully
curving, laying out, settling softly, lightly
on the skin of the water.

I see him in the double house on Alhambra Street, in his den,
trapped forever, condemned to work a lathe at Picker X-Ray,
to spend his nights turning in that chair, around and around
in his dream on Alhambra Street,

turning, turning,
my Uncle Freddy,
and I hear him saying:
Pow!

He says:
Pow!

ANTOINE ON HUNTING AND SOME SPOOKS

David, you go hauntin'? I be.
Now I got annuder moud to feed.
Gonna plug a gov'ment beef.
Don't care if it be a skipper needer.
I ain't haunt dem hardwood ra'bits
since I was a boy, since dat time one fall
dose downcountry killers stay to our place.
T'ree of 'em, all out back tagedder in a baunch,
see a big ol' bauck, all fire to once,
fill dat poor ol' basterd up,
but he keep on goin', jomp over da fence,
hang all his gut out on da wire
but keep goin'. Poor ol' basterd.
Whan I see dat, I quit. Dunno why.

I haf' a version of dat deer dat night,
see him in my dream just like a spook.
He keep on raunin', den he turn araoun'
an' raun right thru dem basterds
an' keep on goin'.
I still see 'im all dese years afder
and' he *still* goin'.

Dat make me t'ink about our haunted house.

When I be a pup we caum daown fraum Derby
move to our place.

Da ol' spooks don' like da way we put da furniture.
We lay in bed a' night an' hear 'em daown da stairs
movin' da furniture araound da way dey like it.
We have da priest caum over bless da house;
he say spooks is friendly
all dey wan' is for da furniture
to be da way dey like it.
So we let 'em put it where dey wan'
an' ever't'ing be okay. Julluk 'at.

Only ol' Babe Williams never caum into da house.
He work daown to da cemetery too many years.
He wear 'is hat to bed to keep da spooks out.
He caum over to our place
haf'ta give 'im supper on da porch.
Won't caum in.

Now ol' Babe is dead 'n' gone
just like dat old bauck
an' naow I see 'em bod' tagedder in my dream.

Just last night I seen 'em raunin' side by side
up da road. See right tru em bot'.
You'd t'ink dat be a scary dream
but it wan't.
I like to see 'em raunin' der tagedder.

An' dey was talkin' to each odder
while dey ran.

✦ ✦ ✦

JIMMY

Jimmy is thirty, an only child, still lives at home
with his mother and his father and works the farm with them.
I might never have known him if my car hadn't broken down
one time just outside East Judevine. Jimmy stopped
and fixed it. We got to be sort of friends.
I don't see him all that much but when I do
we visit. We like each other.

At first glance Jimmy looks retarded, but he's not;
it's just that he still moves awkward like a boy.
His head is too big for his body
and his dark eyes and hair—his grandpa's French—
make his round face seem oddly sunken.
He has two fingers missing from one hand,
an accident on the farm.

Jimmy is a good farmer, better than his father,
but probably he'll spend his life working on the home place
and come up to fifty with nothing.
It would be just like his father to die and will the place
to someone else.

When I talk to Jimmy, we always talk about machines.
Jimmy loves machines; he's a good mechanic too,
better than his father.

The one time I saw him dressed up was down at the church
for his uncle's wedding.
He was trying to do the right thing so he walked around
like a tin soldier, a permanent smile pasted on his face.
His fly was down.

When Jimmy talks he holds his hands on edge in the air,
fingers tight together, and moves them in little jerks

from side to side as if
they were fish
trying to swim through grease.
He swallows hard at the end of every phrase.

When you pass him on the road and he waves
he raises his hand flat and forward, fingers still
tight together and his face is stern, almost fearful,
like a Byzantine Jesus offering benediction.

We don't visit all that much but when we do it's hard for me
because
there is something I always want to ask him, something
I want to blurt out, drop the talk of carburetors
and say: Jimmy, what do you do for sex?

He's thirty, lives at home, upstairs, over his parents' room.
There's no woman for him anywhere. He never goes out.
His parents never take him anywhere.
He never sees any of his old high-school friends,
if he ever had any.

I want to say, Jimmy! I want to know. Do you still take
your penis in your hand? How often? Where? In your room
after mother and father have gone to sleep? Do you ride
your snow machine into the woods and do it there?
Don't you want a woman? When you go down to Morrisville
to the feed store where that girl works at the counter,
when you could reach over, touch her—
what do you think about?
Is milking cows dawn and dark enough for you?
Is your snow machine enough?
Do you ever dream of something else?

Or maybe you are happy. Maybe you like it there at home.
What's so very wrong with that?

Or is it, Jimmy, in your thirty years you've come to be
a kind of slave, a eunuch,
in the fields of your lord
and father.

ENVOY TO JIMMY

First I've got to tell you
there's only one radio station around here
anybody ever listens to
because it's the one with the farm news
and the local news and the Trading Post
and comes on at five so folks have music to milk cows by.

Everybody listens to it while they're going down the road.
It's nice because
everybody's head bounces to the same tempo.

I was coming home one day up the river road
and saw Jimmy coming toward me in the pickup
headed for the sawmill or the feed store.

I was going to toot and wave, I always do,
mostly everybody does. Then I saw him
in the cab in that instant
as we passed each other
his arms stretched straight against the wheel,
his head thrown back, eyes almost closed,
his mouth   wide   with song.

ALBERT

Like Edith says:
Albert Putvain's a no good wuthless pup,
ain't too swift neither.
When he was clearin' land 'raound his trailer
he caught the corner of the place wi' the crawler blade
an' tore the bedroom off.
But that ain't nathin', when he was young he and his brother
was workin in the woods
an' Albert backed a crawler right up over top his brother,
squashed 'im flat, killed 'im,
an' it ain't never seemed ta bother Albert any.

Why, he don't know when ta quit.
Him sixty-five and a fifth wife an' a baby girl.
Why, he's got kids from here ta Brattleboro.
Prab'ly the on'y thing he ever learned ta do
so he jes' keeps doin' it.

An' those tew ol' state guys he boards up in that ol' bus,
poor re-tards,
they'd be better off back daown to the hospital,
an Albert sayin':
Ah mik 'im walk da woads so dey won't git wazy.
Why, you know he's makin' money off that thing,
you know he is.
Albert knows more ways a makin' money doin' nathin'
'an the whole rest athe world put together.
But they c'ught 'im too, didn't they?
Last year, one week, got convicted thirteen times
of welfare frawd.

Albert is also an architect.
He has garnished his trailer, as many people do,
with porches and sheds and lean-tos and a garage

so that now you can't even see the trailer
it's so buried in the rubble of his invention.

He has an old hay knife painted silver suspended from wires
hanging over the garage door and a silver sickle and a
silver milk can with a gilded colonial eagle perched
on top of it. In the dooryard there is a whorl
of flower pots with plastic red and white carnations
hanging from the tines of an old hay rake.

Watching over all of this are six pink flamingos
on wire legs, each standing and nodding in the wind.
And out front, perpendicular to the road,
so you can see it good,
there's a hand painted sign that glows in the dark
and says:

Mr. Putvain.

THE TWO OLD GUYS AT ALBERT'S

There are two retarded guys from the state hospital
boarded in a bus at Albert's. I don't know their names.
Nobody does. Albert never takes them anywhere.
Maybe the state told him not to; I don't know.
It's not much. An old bus to sleep in, nothing to do
but walk the road and shovel snow, bounce a ball
for Albert's kid in the afternoon, listen to each other
masturbate at night. Not much, but better than the hospital.

The ward   a room   crowded with fifty beds
twenty-five on either wall.   The old men who lie   all day
on their sides   all facing   the same way
so no one has to face   another.   Their only cooperation.

The old men who lie   all day   and say nothing
look at   nothing.   The kid   fourteen   who rocks all day
in a chair   that doesn't rock.   Cold coffee
from a peanut butter jar.   The smell of men
who wet their pants.   Stale tobacco air.   Dark halls.
And doors   locked doors.   The moans at night.
And once a day   the doctor
with a hypodermic.

The manic girl across the courtyard   who every day
takes down her pants   and dances   jangling
like a crow   across the porch   crying   like a crow:
Hey Baby!   Hey Baby!   Come over here!
She lifts her dress   and puts   fingers
between her legs   and rubs   twitching   like a crow
until she falls   her wings spread out   her body
shivering   on the porch floor.

You   watching through the window   your penis
in your hands   in a room with fifty others
rubbing   rubbing   while you watch   and while
the attendant   watches you.
Then your hand is sticky   smelling of ammonia.
You wipe it on your pants   front and back
strop it   like a razor.

I have seen men jailed in rooms   all of them   so lost
so alone   that there is nothing—
not a summer rain   not a smile   not a doughnut—
to be shared.   Men like particles of dust suspended
in the air   floating   at random   making
accidentally   without purpose   action and reaction
to no end   men   (like me)   moving   isolated
dumb   unknowing   suspended in the air.

There are these two retarded guys boarded up at Albert's.

You can see them every day walking the road between
their bus and where the hill starts up to Granny's.

The younger one, who looks about fifteen but probably is forty,
tilts and limps as he walks. His mouth
is permanently distorted and his misshapen head shows
that if he ever had a mother
she didn't care enough to roll him in his crib
so his head wouldn't flatten in the back.
When I wave to him he jerks his arm up, stops,
turns his ugly face and smiles.
Then quick, as if someone hollered at him,
he goes on walking,
tilting and limping and walking.

I wonder if he dreams about the manic girl,
if he still sees her in the night,
jangling in her bones, dancing, crying for him
like a crow.

The older one who looks, and probably is, fifty-five
walks straight but keeps his arms out from his sides
stiff and at an angle.
His hands flutter constantly.
When I wave to him his roadside arm rises and falls,
rises and falls,
with the hand fluttering at its end,
but his eyes stay down on the road.
I have never seen his face.
The old guy keeps that up, the arm rising and falling,
the hand trembling at its end.
I can see it in the rearview mirror until I make the bend.

There are two retarded guys boarded up at Albert's.
Every day they walk the road.
They never walk together.

They are always
about a hundred feet apart.

GRANNY

Granny lived down the road from Albert.
She was eighty when she died. Everybody said she was crazy.
Probably she was. She was suspicious of everyone.
She had visions, saw conspiracies, thought every stranger
who came along was out to get her.
She always liked me because I waved when I went by.

Granny had a cleft palate and no teeth.
She was also hard-of-hearing
so when she talked to you she shouted.
Her husband died about ten years ago.
The winter he died the house burnt down.
Granny spent the last decade of her life alone
living in a springhouse and a camper trailer.
She milked ten cows every day, twice a day,
to the day she died.
She was obsessed with the memory of her husband, Lee.
She talked about him constantly
and when she did
she moaned a nasal, toothless, hair-lipped moan.

Granny had a dream of selling out, moving
to Morrisville to manage an apartment building.
She lived her dream and sold her place about twice a year.
She'd have a lawyer draw a deed and bill of sale,
then at exactly the last moment, she'd back out.
Nobody ever had the heart, thank God,
to make her follow through.
Everybody understood how Granny was.

Once a guy from Hardwick
who didn't know what buying land from Granny really meant
actually got a cattle truck of Holsteins to the barn.
The neighbors could see what was coming
so we stopped by to watch the show.
The guy climbed down out of the cab all smiles.
Granny was waiting for him, the bill of sale in her hand.
She hollered something at him about her husband,
then lit the bill of sale and threw it at him.
After that she didn't sell the place so much.

Granny couldn't leave. The day the house burnt down
Lee's ghost left the house and went to living in the barn.
She couldn't leave Lee's ghost.

Granny never did anybody any harm.

A few years ago, in August, after haying,
a woman we had met at a party in Craftsbury came to see us.
She had a kid with her, a guy about eighteen.
They were driving an old Pontiac station wagon.
There were four dogs in the back.
They parked at the foot of the drive.
The car's shocks were gone and even after they got out,
the car still bobbed and shivered in its place
like a tin behemoth with Parkinson's disease.

They staggered up the hill to the house.
They were high or drunk or both.
It was ten o'clock in the morning.
We drank some of their wine; then they drove off
down the road toward the village.

Later I found out they stopped at Granny's place.
Granny was in the pasture
graining a heifer she had staked under a maple tree.

They jumped out of the car
and ran across the pasture to the old woman.
She was a total stranger to them.
They hugged her and kissed her and shouted wildly:
Power to the people! Power to the people!
They told Granny they were going to give her lots of money
and that she'd never have to work again.
Granny broke away from them and ran into the barn
and hid in the hayloft. Bobbie found her up there
that evening after dark.

The woman from Craftsbury and her friend came back
once more that summer.
This time Granny was in the barn when they pulled up.
She ran out the back, across the pasture, through a swamp
and hid in the high grass of Rufus Chaffee's orchard
all afternoon.

Granny died last spring, in the morning
while she was doing chores.
Bobbie found her about noon, lying in the gutter,
the milking machine still pulsating in her hand
and the cows blatting from the pain of stretched udders.

I miss Granny. I miss her angry voice.
I miss her plaintive wail for Lee.

I remember the first time I ever met Granny.
I was bucking firewood one fall, some maples
the power company had let down
along the lane into Uncle Clyde's.
Granny shuffled over from her trailer on the hill.
She was furious.

'ut 'er 'ooin! 'ew 'ow 'ut 'er 'ooin?
'ems 'ah 'ees! 'oo 'ol 'ew 'ew 'ou'd 'ut 'em?

'ut 'er 'ooin! 'ems 'ah 'ees!
'iss 'ah 'an', ain't 'yde's!
I 'ew 'ief 'ee?
Ah'm an ol' 'oman, 'even'y-'ix 'ears ol'
'ah 'us'un's 'ead. 'ah 'oaus 'urnt ou'.
'ah 'if a'on i' a 'ing'oaus an' a 'ailer,
'ah 'ik 'en 'aows.
'ah əh 'et i!

I apologized. Told her I didn't mean to steal her trees.
Said I thought they were Clyde's. Granny mellowed
and ended telling me I was welcome to the wood.

'er 'el'um 'ew 'at 'ood.
ah'm 'ad 'er 'ew 'ew 'ave ih.
Ih 'ew 'eed ih, ah'm 'ad 'er 'ew 'ew 'ave ih.
'er 'ik'd on 'iss 'ill. Ah 'een 'ew 'o i.
'ew 'ave.
'er 'ik'd on 'iss 'ill.
Ah'm 'ad 'er 'ew 'ew 'ave ih.

Then she began about her husband, Lee.
It was the first time I'd ever heard her lament.
Her vowels elongated. She lengthened all her final sounds,
syncopated all her phrases. She moaned. She wailed.
She rolled her head and sang.

Oh, ah 'ish   'ew'd 'et   ah 'us'un', 'ee!
'ee uz ah 'icest 'an   'at e'er 'od   in 'ews!
'ee um 'alkin' 'oun ah 'oad   un 'ay,   'opped in
'an 'e'er 'eft.
'ow 'e's 'ead!
Ah 'us'un's 'ead!
An' ah'm an ol' 'woman,   'even'y-'ix 'ears ol',
ah 'us'un's 'ead!
Ah 'oaus 'urnt ou',

ah 'if a' on i' a 'ing'oaus an a 'ailer,
ah 'ik 'en 'aows,
ah əh 'et i!

Ah 'us'un's 'ead!
'ee's 'ead!

an ah'm   a'oun!

A TRANSCRIPTION OF GRANNY'S MONOLOGUES

What you doing! You know what you're doing?
Them's my trees! Who told you you could cut them?
What you doing! Them's my trees!
This my land, ain't Clyde's!
Why you grief me?
I'm an old woman, seventy-six years old.
My husband's dead. My house burnt out.
I live alone in a springhouse and a trailer.
I milk ten cows.
I just get by!

◆

You're welcome to that wood.
I'm glad for you to have it.
If you need it, I'm glad for you to have it.
You're liked on this hill. I seen you go by.
You wave.
You're liked on this hill.
I'm glad for you to have it.

◆

Oh, I wish   you'd met   my husband, Lee.

49

He was the nicest man   that ever trod   in shoes.
Lee come walking down the road   one day   stopped in
and never left.
Now he's dead!
My husband's dead!
And I'm an old woman,   seventy-six years old
my husband's dead.
My house burnt out,
I live alone in a springhouse and a trailer.
I milk ten cows,
I just get by!

My husband's dead!
Lee's dead!

And I'm   alone!

✦ ✦ ✦

FORREST

Forrest died five years ago.
I never really knew him.
But I saw him, almost daily, winter and summer,
flapping down the Dunn Hill road toward the family graves
up where Hermie used to live.

I could see him loping,
taking those huge strides as if he were
angrily running after
a child,
his old gray overcoat dragging
on the gravel,

and that World War One
aviator's hat
flapping at his ears.

GOING PLACES

Eighty-six years ago Forrest squeezed between his mother's thighs
and stayed   on the farm   where he arrived,   and he died
where he was born:
A life of work and watching in that place,
the same house, same view out the windows,
same sidehill pasture, garden, fields and barn,
woodlot, brook and meadow.

*According to our way of thinking, the Zapotecs were crazy not to make
use of the wheel when they knew of its existence. The curious thing is that
they had wheels, but only for toys. . . . They were in a word perfectly
capable of "inventing the wheel" but for some reason (which must remain*

*to us profoundly mysterious) they never bothered with it. They were not
interested in going places.*

Thomas Merton
Ishi Means Man

He grew there, became a man, took over, married,
raised a family, traveled widely over his two hundred acres,
but never left the state.

Except that once,
a downcountry friend took him to the ocean in Connecticut.
He walked across the beach to the edge of continent and sea,
dipped his fingers in the surf, tasted of it, turned and said:
It's salty. Let's go home.

Except for that he hardly left the county.

Zapotec or neighbor, three thousand years ago in Mexico
or yesterday just down the road, the image clings,
proof of our dissatisfaction, our longing
for a time when going places didn't mean a thing,
when we could do our work and know
some comfort in our skins.

SARAH

It wasn't Sarah's idea to come up here. Timothy's the one
who wanted to quit a good job in the bank,
give up his suits and ties and dress shoes
and go north into the wilderness so he could fulfill some kind of
boy's dream of working in the woods.

Sarah had been happy where she was, in Connecticut, or happy
    enough, if happiness has anything to do with it,
but she'd come nevertheless out of obligation or indifference,

she didn't know, nor did she care.

All she knew was, she was here now, dumped out here in the
    middle of nowhere.
All day alone in that old farmhouse while Timothy
staggered around in the snowy woods in his boots and heavy shirts
and coveralls reeking of gas and oil, sweat and pitch.
Not exactly what Sarah had had in mind for the rest of her life.

In the hours of her isolation and her loneliness, day after day,
Sarah became aware that she was more than merely bored.
Her life was meaningless, without a purpose, which struck her
    oddly
that she would worry over such things as purpose and meaning
since such concerns were not a part of the material and
    consumptive, self-indulgent lap of opulence
out of which she had come.

Then Sarah realized that these new and odd concerns had come to
her because of her friendship with Ann and Raymond.

Raymond and Ann farmed a small farm on the other side of the
    hill, and on the far side of huge and desolate Bear Swamp.
Raymond and Ann were kind and warm, open and generous,
and when Timothy and Sarah first arrived
they took the two young people into their lives
and made them feel wanted and at home.

At first it was Timothy who leapt into the friendship learning
    from them
all he could about gardening, wood heat, the myriad details of
    how to live
in the country and in the north. But as time passed and Timothy
had gotten from them what he wanted, he lost interest in them,
while Sarah, for reasons at first she couldn't understand, initiated

an ever-deepening contact
with the older couple.

As Sarah grew more and more attached to Raymond and Ann,
    she began to think of them as trees
rooted and growing in that place, these two
whose lives seemed so considered and complete, as if their lives
were a dream of what human life could be.

In the afternoons when she is alone in her house,
Sarah goes into the bedroom,
opens the curtains across the window that looks out on the
meadow and the mountains,
lies down on the bed and stares across the snowy fields,
the blank and empty whiteness,
into the purpling winter afternoon,
and she weeps,
for the loneliness she feels, for the emptiness she knows,
which is so much greater than the emptiness beyond the window.

Timothy tired of his childhood dream and went back to
    Connecticut,
back to the bank, but Sarah stayed on alone in Judevine.

After a time a young man moved in with Sarah, stayed awhile,
and then was gone. Then there was another and another.

Then a woman came to stay whose name was Breeze Anstey.
Breeze and Sarah started an herb farm and sustained
their business and their life together for a few years,
but that liaison ended also, and Sarah, as she had done before,
stayed on alone.

RAYMOND AND ANN

I

Raymond and Ann kept to themselves and because of that
some people thought them snooty and aloof. It wasn't true.
Other people theorized perhaps there'd been
some great pain in their lives, more than
the stillborn child buried on the knoll
above their house, that kept them from the usual
sociability. No one knew. Personally, I think when they came
to this mountain fifty years ago they wanted
only silence and each other and having found
these things they were happy.

Raymond was God's gardener. He grew the best of everything,
his garden always free of weeds, rows so straight
it seemed he planted with a transit.

Although they were poor and everything about the place
homemade, their farm had neatness and an order
reflective of people who know what to do and how to do it
and who do not overstretch the limits of their land
or themselves.

By the time I knew them they were old and didn't have a team,
only Sandy, middling size, mostly Belgian, who weighed
maybe seventeen hundred pounds and was so intelligent
if she'd had hands she would have harnessed herself,
intuited the day's work and done her jobs unattended.
I always had the feeling that, though there were other animals—
cows, chickens, sheep, a pig—there was an absolute equality
between the man, the woman, and the horse.

Raymond was tall, angular and bony.
He carried himself upright to his dying day.

He cackled when he laughed and when he told a joke
he always laughed *before* the punch line
so he could be the first.

Ann was slim and quick, full breasts and hips,
and although her face was plain, she was to me
unspeakably beautiful. She wore her white hair
and wrinkled skin the way a summer flower wears its bloom.
And in her eyes, even at the age of seventy, burnt a fire
so bright and fierce, a passion so intense,
it made me feel old and worn. In her presence
I was sick at the slackness of my life.

II

Every afternoon after dinner Raymond and Ann
lay down together on the large sofa in the living room,
wrapped themselves around each other and took a nap.

Sometimes they slept, sometimes they only lay
in the stillness listening. In summer they listened
to the wind and the birds' songs. In winter
they listened to the wind and the mute birds—little feet
scuttling across the feeder on the windowsill. Often
they fell into a half-sleep in which they dreamed
waking dreams or they let their minds go still as the room.

They napped like this each day because it was a time
when they could come together, these two distinctly separate
people, touch each other and be very nearly one being
in that place.

They had an unspoken understanding that during these times
they wouldn't talk, but one day Ann said: You know,
we've been more than fifty years, doing the same things
day after day, changing only with the seasons and I've never

got tired of it, oh, angry and frustrated, plenty,
but never tired. I wonder if we ever will.

Raymond chuckled: Well, we had better get to it
if we're going to; we don't have much time left.

They both saw clearly and briefly then
the end of their lives and they laughed quietly
and held each other.

III

I was thinking just now, Raymond said, about that time,
years ago, after we built this place. I could see the two
of us lying on the sofa and I remembered clearly how we looked
and what I thought. We were young and new and I held you here
as we are now and I was thinking, I wonder what it will be like
to be here when we're old, the two of us in shrinking bodies
wrapped around each other. I think I knew then, fifty years ago,
pretty clearly what it would be like today. I knew
how it would feel. Do you think that means our lives
have been too predictable?

Why should it?

Well, to see that far ahead and then get to where you saw
and look back and see you were right
seems so strange, predictable.

Have you enjoyed it?

You know I have.

I have too.

IV

Toward the end of the sixties and into the early seventies
every summer there was what Antoine called a "hippie invasion"
around here. Young people from the cities poured into
these hills. I remember one spring Antoine saying:

Watch out! boys. Dere really caumin' in dis summer.
Dere's gonna be a million of 'em wash in here like a tidal
wa'f. Dis place use' to be more caows 'an people,
now we're gonna be more hippies 'an caows!

Raymond and Ann became mentors to them,
elders with Confucian knowledge, replacements
for the parents the kids had left behind.
Raymond and Ann were visions of another way of life.

But the influence went both ways and Raymond took
to working in the garden barefooted,
then he went shirtless and got a summer tan,
then he removed his cap and the traditional
bronzed forehead with abrupt demarcation
between the sunburn and the ashen skull disappeared.
It was the talk of the town. What was he doing
at sixty-something acting like a kid?
It tickled Ann, and what other people said
didn't bother her at all. It never had.

One summer afternoon Raymond came in from the garden,
approached Ann from behind, put his arms around her middle
and kissed the back of her neck. Then his forearms touched
her breasts dangling unsupported beneath her shirt.
And her shirt was open from the top a few buttons.

Goodness, what is this?

58

What is what?

This.

His hands moved to her breasts and held them.

Well, maybe you shouldn't be thinking you're the only one
can learn from hippies. If you go around with half your clothes
still on the hook, I guess I can leave half mine in the drawer.

Well, I guess you can!

Raymond rested his chin on her shoulder
and gazed down her shirt.

Does it feel good?

Sort of strange would be more like it.

Do you like it?

Some.

Would you go out in public the way you are right now?

Raymond Miller, you know I'm not a hussy!

V

They were under the dooryard apple tree at the summer table
shelling peas when they heard the noise.
Early July, the height of summer, clear and warm
and a light breeze to stir things, cool things,
an idle day filled with ease, gentle and sweet
and a rarity in this ungentle place.
A half-dozen days a year like this, no more, the others

always with some kind of edge to them, a harshness,
which makes it all the more wonder-filled that this place
could yield two people such as Ann and Raymond.

At first a dull roar in the distance, then closer and louder
until when it passed through the sugarbush just down the road,
it had to it the sound of war. Then they were there:
four of them. Four steel helmets gleaming black,
four faces with dark glasses, four faces pale, ashen, as if
they had been powdered. In black they came:
black leather jackets, leather pants, leather boots,
leather gloves with gauntlets to the elbows and silver rivets
gleaming everywhere, their bikes black and silver too—
choppers, handlebars in the air, seats leaning back—
they roared into the lane and toward the house and garden.

The chickens scratching in the dooryard screamed
and ran away; Sandy reared and bolted, broke through the fence
and disappeared into the woods.

In black they came, into the garden, into the rows of corn,
over tomatoes, down rows of broccoli, through the fence of peas.
They wheeled and turned and came again, through the garden
    flowers,
over squash and cucumbers, dill and thyme, carrots, potatoes,
beans. One rider singled out an errant hen and ran her down.
They came again through the garden, their tires
churning and digging the earth, spewing soil and broken plants
into the air. They roared toward the two old people
then veered away, down the lane, down the road,
over the hill and away.

VI

After supper on a summer evening.
They were sitting in the cool house, she in his easy chair.

She looked up at him quizzically; already she had left him,
was in a strange place, alone. He watched the life
drain from her face. She said nothing—
not even good-bye.

He sat for a time in the growing dusk and stillness.
Then, as the sun headed down behind the mountains,
he scooped her into his arms the way you would a child
fallen asleep somewhere away from its bed and laid her down
on the sofa where she liked to nap.

He went to the barn and finished chores,
then stepped into the evening and felt the cold air
spilling down the sidehill all around him. He listened
to the crickets, the barred owl and white-throated sparrow,
the wood thrush. Then he came inside and went to bed.

In the first light of morning he dug a grave on the knoll
behind the house next to the child's grave, then went to the barn
and built a box of rough pine boards from his store of lumber.
He harnessed Sandy and she drug the box to the knoll
and with her help he lowered it into the grave.

He went into the house and picked her up. He wrapped his arms
around her middle and carried her upright, her head rising above
his head because she was stiff.
He put her in the box, put on the lid and nailed it down.
He covered her over. He filled the grave.

He sat down on the freshly mounded earth
and began rocking slowly back and forth.
And then he wept.
His tears poured down. He moaned and wailed.
He rolled his head and wept.
He shook his fist at heaven. He rose and paced and wept.
He held his face in his hands. He clawed his pants,
tore at his shirt. He stomped the earth and smashed a fist

into an open palm. He turned his face toward heaven
clinched his teeth
and screamed.

When there were no tears left, when he was weak and trembling,
he led Sandy to the barn, unharnessed her,
turned her out to pasture
and went into the house.

He stood at the window then, looking at the mountains,
and he wept again,
this never-ending, accumulated grief
for the inevitable.

POEM FOR A MAN WHOSE WIFE HAS DIED

You can see him in his house
sitting in a chair
his hands folded in his lap
his mouth slightly open.

You can see him in his house
standing at a window
one hand of fingers touched gently
to his lower lip.

You can see him in his house
moving from room to room
his hand trailing his wife's ghost
like a child's blanket.

✦ ✦ ✦

CRAZY TWO-FOOT MAKES IT ROUND AGAIN

The year turns toward itself until it joins itself
and makes beginning end. It makes a circle not a line,
and held within that closure, in the crush of breaths and flesh
is a man, turning in the turning year, bending as all breaths bend
toward the dead, his flesh toward soil.

NOVEMBER

Where do you enter a circle?
When there is no beginning where do you break in?
Say November. Here. Enter through the emptiness.

Sere gray. Sere brown. The bare trees,
their skinny fingers darkened by the rain, stretch
against the sky. The earth is dank and chill
as an old deserted cellar. Barren. Without song.
The sky is empty, the birds are gone.
Everything is waiting in the rain.

Five o'clock: almost dark. Chimney smoke lies down,
crawls across the meadow like a slow, soft snake.
And he, just come in from the woods, stands watching.
The cold fog is silver on his woolen shirt.

Bank on bank of clouds, like the folds of a shroud,
layer over the mountains.
The sky steals light from both ends of the day.
This is the day the lead gray sky comes down.
Say good-bye to the ground. In the morning: white.
It will snow all night tonight.

DECEMBER

Where there was darkness there is light.
See how morning floods his house.
See the sunlight bounding off the snowy earth,
leaping through the windows. How could such dark create
this bright and lucid day? This must be another place.
It couldn't be the same.

Cold and crystal air. There!
Ravens catch the wind and soar
like hawks.
Blonk. Blonkblonk.
Blonk. Blonk.

Further on toward evening, in the dying light, a human figure
ambles down the road, his hands jammed deep into his pockets,
his white breath streaming behind him like a scarf.

Snow. Featherfluff. Enough to crush the world.
Of itself on itself, layer on layer white.

One fence post tilts above the snow.
The tip of a ship gone down
in this white sea.

JANUARY

Mid night: moon bright:
minus twenty-two degrees
and the man
walks the swamp road to feel
the hair in his nostrils freeze.

Crack and crunch.
A dog lopes across the crusted moonlit snow.
From his jaw a deer leg bobs and dangles.

In the silver dark chimney smoke rises
a hundred feet toward the Pleiades
then flattens to a T.

In the middle of the bright and moony night
bobcat comes to drink the spring's clear water.

No cloud for weeks. He can see the stars at noon.
The moon-cold sun burns for nothing.
A white desert: arid: still.

Red polls scratch and twitter.
Snow buntings rise and swirl and blow away.

Far now the other side of solstice:
forty below and growing colder.
The sound of popping trees.

FEBRUARY

Five o'clock and not yet dark. He sits in the silent house,
drinking tea and watching stove light flow like quiet water.
Everything is old. In the cellar, squash mold, potatoes sprout,
onions fall in upon themselves. And this human flesh too:
brittle as the frozen trees. Beginning at the bottom of his heel
the skin falls powdery on the floor as if flesh really were dust.

If a white cat has one blue eye it'll be
deaf.
If in the middle of the winter the spiders down cellar hang down
it'll be
an early spring.

He saw a snowy owl this evening, the two of them come upon
    each other at the end of a day of hunting.
She was sitting on a branch of a tree watching him.
He stopped. They stared at each other; then she
rolled backward off the branch and disappeared
into the darkening trees.

Six o'clock and almost dark. Some animals turn homeward,
others just waking slip into the evening.
Somewhere beyond the meadow
a deer stands up in her snowy bed suddenly afraid.

Too dark. Too cold. Too long. Blue jay, glutton, garish crab,
blue knife of madness, shrieks at the morning.
His cries stab and shatter across the ice.

MARCH

Rain-glaze on snow. Mud and ice and snow.
Coyotes feed themselves on gaunt dreams of spring. Then
what comes slowly suddenly he sees.

Light hovers longer in the southern sky.
Brooks uncover themselves. Alders redden.
Grosbeaks' beaks turn green. Chickadee finds the song
he lost last November, and blue jay abandons
argument and gluttony. He cranes his neck,
bobs his mitered head; he bounces on a naked branch
crying: Spring!
But, like all winter's keepers,
he speaks his dream before
he sees the fact.
Did you hear a phoebe?

And he out again and walking on the earth,
in the air, in the sun, ankle deep in mud.

APRIL

Still no green but slowly now
earth softens to the touch.
Buds stand up like nipples.
The sun beats down.
The death robes shrink
like cellophane before the fire.
Mountain brooks make rage of melting snow.

In the dooryard, the ghosts of winter's grimy rubble rise
like demented souls on Judgment Day:
Glass and rusting cans, broken tires, potato peels, a carburetor,
coffee grounds, tea bags, crankcase oil, a tail pipe, bacon grease,
a hubcap bowl of oily water, wood chips,
a thousand dog turds on the lawn,
plastic bags, onion skins,
the lower jaw of last year's slaughtered pig,
a broken plate, sodden cardboard boxes, gravel on muddy grass,
two deflated pumpkins. The yard is a notebook
where winter's journal wrote itself in litter.

Yet also still this dank and gray. Oh, how he loves
this cold and constant rain, this gray spring,
the chill that keeps him indoors
and the fire going in the stove all day.

He loves this last nod toward the passing dark.
he loves all that is empty, slothful and withdrawn,
this time in which he has a few more days
to stay within himself, and be quiet in his melancholy.

He loves these last days of the barren time
before he has to go outside
and greet the redolent and noisy spring.

Wind and rain.
A rush of wings.
The trees loud again with birds.

Birch and popple catkins droop:
spent penises drip yellow semen
on the air.

Popple and red maple push new leaves.

The geese return.
Their long vees plow the fields of cloud.
High and far away, they are
strange, mysterious as new leaves.

Below them, chickadee, like a friendly hand, remains:
close, diminutive, minimal, half-forgotten
in the bare apple tree.

MAY

In the morning white-throated sparrow cries: The sun! The sun!
I bring the sun in the bright spot beside my eye.
Come out! Come out of your house! The sun has come!

Oh, spring and sun! Song and wing.
The earth redolent of everything!
Including death.

The worst endured, last year's fawn seeks a southern slope,
lays her starven body down and dies in the warming sun.

Wind and rain. Wind and rain to shag, loosen, stiffened hearts.
Wind and rain. Wind and rain to rot the corpse.

Gorged, glutted, water-mad the mountain brook
meets the winter-weakened doe takes her, tears her, reddens itself
then scatters the scraps of hide and bone. Tossed up away
the limpid foetus-bones lie caged inside mother's cradle ribs.
Next year's adder's-tongue will sprout
from the empty socket of its eye.
Above a mist, a spirit, like primordial steam streams upward
through the warming rain.

In the woods too. Wolf tree. Den tree. Where the roots go in.
Raccoon, her chin resting softly on crossed paws, her eyes
looking straight ahead: dead.

The earth is pimpled with the dead. These rotting corpses are
her body's phosphorescent jewels. No matter. No matter.
Fertilizer now. All done. Make more with earth and rain and sun.

Earth says to sun: Come seed, come! And he,
hands filled with seed,
moves over the freshly turned earth planting peas and spinach.

Skunk cabbage spears the muck: a furled tip, an artist's brush.
Who's under there? What arm will follow handle?
What mad painter rise to smear the world with green?

Now the round-leafed violet comes, the first point of light,
a yellow mite above the grimy leaves.
And dogtooth violet—trout lily, green-gray, green-brown,
the adder's-tongue—flickers above the ground.
Purple trillium—wake-robin, bloody stinkin' Benjamin—
velvet drapes rich as deer blood coyote spilled on snow.

There. What's left of deer.

No hide. No bone. Just hair
lying soft as milkweed bloom.

Here. The myrtle warbler dressed for spring.
Bright white, blue bright, gray and yellow light,
who doesn't warble at all but cheeps and says:
this is sour, acid soil, is spruce and fir,
is north, is where I make my nest.

There: below him in the wet, brushy place
year after year, generation after generation,
the woodcock whistle and snout.

And there: on only slightly higher ground
the veeries, dreaming they are falling water,
warble and sing their liquid descending glissando,
year after year.

And year after year
always again in the same place
the partridge drums.

And here almost beside him the shy junco
scurries, flits across the ground singing
again this spring only: *tick, tick, tick, tick.*

Lilacs in the dooryard bloom.
The air is sweet as honied tea.
The orchard hums.

JUNE

Seeds break ground. Stretch up. Stretch down.

Now each morning before the sun

two ravens, rulers of the dawn, the sun's black acolytes,
come croaking crying: Day!

Today they saw him watching: a sudden silence:
they wheeled: the hiss and rush of wings.
Gone, withered into the rising sun. And he,
left standing, growing that day's dying shadow.

It is light half the night. It's always day. The sun won't go away.
And green. Darkening green.
The flowers of the world dancing on jade slate.

Cloistered under earth's fertile skin,
the cabbage seed hides a dream of growing inside out,
swelling outward from an inner fire, from
a core tightening daily around its secret heart.

A black fisher cat walked across a black log this morning
his black coat silver in the sunny fog.

JULY

Now each morning, each warm morning,
sunlight on the dew-wet grass, sunlight
on the garden, everything under the sun in these
brief, salubrious days of life and juice and green.

In the steaming swamp in the middle of the day
the snowshoe hare
all brown and summery
cocks his head, listens, scratches lice behind his ear.

In the evening the man stands in his garden and watches the
    vegetables and thinks:
if this group of animals to which he belongs had decided,

in an act of selflessness, of generosity and distance from their idea
of themselves, that the supreme act of creativity and intelligence
    was not to make language or history but instead
to make food by photosynthesis,
why, then, this blue-green broccoli here every day more greatly
    stretching toward the sun would be
the ultimate, the pinnacle, the very top
of the pyramid of being!

He sweats: hayseed stuck in eye-crotch, arm-crotch, crotch.
He stinks, a sweet, thick stink. He loves himself the way he stinks.

Later, because such things happen, suddenly, where field meets
    swamp, without his knowing,
the tractor's cutter bar slipped
under the frightened, frozen bittern and bit her legs—off.
The legless bittern flies away pouring blood across the withering
    grass. She flies away to no perch, to no leg
to stand on.

Two green-and-ruby hummingbirds.
His red shirt.
A flare of yellow lilies.

Blue-eyed grass: green spear and violet eye, a point of yellow iris.

Green pasture.
Orange hawkweed.
Yellow buttercups.

Up before the sun, wading through the bramble
dropping dew-wet, bright red berries into a metal cup.

Oh, praise this life! Praise this world!
Praise and joy for being here—
here with all these others! Alive and here! Praise for all of us!

For everyone!

Hot summer afternoon and he
in the cool and darkened shade of his woodshed
sitting cross-legged on the floor a sharpening stone in his hand
putting an edge on a hoe and from time to time drinking
from his cup of tea and thinking how since time began
men have paused
in the heat of a summer afternoon to rest in the shade
to sharpen a tool, to drink tea.

Then the F-111 flew low over the house and in his dream
he saw a Vietnamese farmer sitting cross-legged in a hut also
on a hot summer afternoon also resting in the shade and also
sharpening a tool and from time to time
drinking from his cup of tea.
And then, in his dream, he saw the other man's house, his family,
his fields, his self all consumed in flames, all—gone
as if they had been washed away in a wave of fire.

And when the man woke from his dream he saw that not himself
nor his family nor his house nor his fields nor any thing
that is there in that place
had been consumed, only his heart consumed in the fire
of his rage.

The next day in the garden he looked at the cabbages and saw
    human skulls.
The beans were disembodied fingers,
the lettuces flaps of human skin,
an ear of corn an unexploded bomb, the squash were land mines
of different shapes and sizes, the tomatoes lumps of bloody flesh
exploding in his hands.

AUGUST

Here: this balsam fir: every internodal, every terminal bud
thousands of them charged with energy and will
seizing the momentary summer
grown thirty inches in sixty days
reaching wildly out
before light fails falls back
drags
cold and dark
over them again.

Slowly the frantic chores of summer wane, the air cools,
and already that autumnal cry of insects floats across the earth—
these fleshy instants of a summer's day plant seed in harvest time
trust their futures to the earth and prepare to go away.

The end of summer and the sun that baked his head
passes coolly now across his shoulders.

Evening:
when day's birds are gone and night's wanderers wait listening
when dark falls softly as a bird's wing, then, beyond the meadow
in the bull spruce a barred owl: *alone   alone   alone*
begins his dark melody to the moon.

In the morning before the dawn
seven heifers
up to their necks in fog
sway and wade supple as cats.

A day of summer rain. Then
in the evening dark it stops and
the moon begins orange and huge
through the branches of the apple tree.

The year, this quick and momentary summer,
tumbles down its long fall toward dark.
Aster and gentian now. The last blue under the sun.

SEPTEMBER

The dawn brings air thin and clear as cellophane.
Under a cloudless sky, the frost passes
through a kingdom that knew only sun and rain,
a gentle people of leaves who ripened fruit all summer.

Tomato corpses droop from assassination stakes, their tender
    bodies riddled by the frost.
The garden is a grave. What vegetables remain
lie fugitive from cold, sequestered underground. Then rain.
Red leaves turn white bellies to the wind.

The year teeters perfectly on light's fulcrum: the equinox.
Then it sinks. In a fog it drowns as in a sea. The varying gray,
the mist, shows each ridge, each spine of mountains separate
from the others, as if row on row of granite breakers caught
in a photograph, in perpetual stillness, might roll again,
might make
a primal, fogbound ocean here—miles from any water.

Now the sun again and the world filling up with color with that
sweet Chinese melancholy in this time of the chrysanthemum.

OCTOBER

A dying time is time to kill. Cow. Chicken. Sheep.
His hands are stained with blood. Carcass on the kitchen table
and he sings softly to himself and scrapes
seven different kinds of flesh
from a pig's skull.

The smell of dying leaves, the slanting light
drive him out to kill again.
This time just for fun. Partridge, drumming bird, watch out!

A warm October afternoon the kind they have in paradise.
The bird, the gun explode. Feather ball falls like a wad of dough.
His small beak, his eyes bleed. He beats his breast and makes
snow angels in the leaves. Strange penance, or is it adulation,
for his life as if to drive out quick what little life is left.

He can kill a rabbit too. Hear the rabbit scream. Hear him squeal.
Every fox for miles will be here soon to find only a tiny pool
of blood, some fur and guts.

The killer lopes home through the sweet October yellow light.
He puckers, whistles, his face bright with sun.
He who is alive in the world with these creatures who are dead,
whose round bodies are soft and limp and warm
in the pocket of his coat.

Hush little babies
don't you cry
leaves die too.

This autumnal sadness.

Starshine.
Cold October night.
Cows.
Knee deep in mist.

Now almost all the leaves are down.
Now the popples turning yellow.
Now and last the tamaracks. Everything becoming gray—again.
Again the bare trees their skinny fingers stretched against the sky.

Last night the sky filled with geese
those voices high and strange
and far away who cried: Good-bye!

The next day: forty degrees and raining.
The earth shivers in its cloudy robe.
Crows swarm and go.

Today, in the wind: a tremolo:
weasel and snowshoe hare
are slowly turning white.
Reflections before the fact.

NOVEMBER AGAIN

Gray. Dark. Return. Chimney smoke lies down
crawls across the meadow like a slow soft snake.

Done. His woodshed full of wood, his little house banked tight
against the cold, the cellar full of meat and vegetables,
he comes inside
and washes blood and summer from his fingernails. In silence now
in the dying year he darkens like the days; he sits and falls,
as leaves fell, deeper into the coming dark, into the time of dream.

Quiet. Quiet. Still.
In the darkening afternoon
watching stove light flicker.

This is the end. The earth is empty again.

The long night steps slowly over the mountains.
The sky steals light from both ends of the day.

PART II

JOURNEY FOR THE NORTH

First, the first white man
ever to arrive and settle in this place speaks,
this man—restless and discontented with where he had been,
wanting
the fulfillment of a vision of what might be.
Then another man speaks,
he who came here for the same reasons 180 years later.

✦

*I left my home in southern Connecticut late in January of 1789 and with
     my wife and two children,
both of whom were girls, the eldest being ten,
I started on my journey for the north
with a team of oxen and one horse, a sledge, and what provisions I had
     deemed necessary for such an undertaking.
About one hundred miles short of our destination one of my oxen failed.
A few days later the horse failed also, and after that I spent most of every
     day in the yoke next to our one remaining animal
and my wife and children walked behind or pushed as was necessary.*

✦

North . . .
to ancient, rounded mountains
all ledge and rock outcropping
yet softened green by forest,
maple, beech, birch, ash and poplar,
larch, spruce, hemlock, cedar, pine
and fir—pointing toward the sky.

✦

*We reached a settlement, now known as Johnson, some twenty-four miles
     west of our final destination toward the end of March
nearly starven and without the horse or ox.*

I had left the downed animals with settlers in the areas where they fell
  with the firm, if vain, hope of returning for them in the spring.

Although I had left Connecticut with numerous tools,
it had been necessary along the way to trade them for the provisions that
  we needed.
When we arrived at our place of residence where we intended to make a
  settlement,
I had only one axe and an old hoe with which to begin clearing land and
  growing crops.
That first summer I cleared about two acres with only an axe, my one
  remaining ox being too sick to be of any help at that time.

✦

Mountains and hill farms, valleys and bottomland
and in the bottom, always, water—
a river or a stream,
white and rocky, slow and muddy,
and in the bottom also, always, villages, because—
gristmill, sawmill, creamery—
power, log course, sewer.

Now, half of what they were a hundred years ago,
but still inhabited
by the beast who sleeps at night and walks upright,
in a landscape overwhelmed still
by something other than
what we have made,
by mountains and valleys,
water and sky, open land
and trees.

◆

*At the time of our settlement this was a wilderness and not the place of
     habitation it is now.*
*To the east it was thirty miles to the nearest human beings, and no road
     but marked trees;*
*to the south, also about thirty miles to the nearest infant settlement, but
     there was no communication with us,*
*and to the north, the woods stretched indefinite, to and beyond the border
     with Canada.*

◆

One village of the many—call it Judevine.
Thirty-six square miles, a billion, billion souls,
six hundred human souls,
two-thirds in the mountains, two hundred in the village,
squeezed between sharp-rising hills,
room only for the highway, railroad, river
and what houses could be put
amongst the three.

And through the valley flows
the river.

◆

*In those early days we were burdened with such a scarce sufficiency as to
     barely support our natures*
and our only respite from continual hunger was what the river gave us.
*Often during a day of clearing land, late in the forenoon, I would faint
     from hunger, whereupon, when I awoke,*
*I would take a fish by angling from the river, broil it on the riverbank, and
     then commence work again.*
*Toward evening I would again take enough fish by angling for myself and
     my family to provide us with that day's only sustenance.*
*We ate these gifts of the river without salt or bread, as we had neither salt
     nor flour at that time.*

83

By the end of our first year in Judevine I had acquired an additional ox by
  laboring in the fields of other men, and we were able
in our second year to plant and harvest enough corn to provide ourselves
  meal for the entire winter.

✦

For a million years
the river raced and languished through this valley
and there were no human souls to see it.
(I wish I'd seen it then.)
Only water and trees and beasts of forest and stream.

Later, Indians, resident here for millennia, a people
and a way of life we know nothing of. And before them . . .
who?

In 1789 we arrived, because . . .
Greed or the desire to be alone, or more likely the yearning
for no constraints, license to do what you will, freedom
from law, society, the obligation to anything but the self—
the wonder and the flaw in our collective personality.

Or was it the dream of the hidden, inner, mystic life
growing in a wilderness, alone, where
inward and outward, other and self, disappear
and the spirit of wholeness rises
definite and sweet as dawn?

✦

Though I was doomed to encounter many additional perils, to suffer
  fatigue and toil on into the future,
our lives began to improve in both character and aspect,
and it seemed to me at that time the Divine Benefactor began rewarding
  me for my labor and my diligence.

The reader will be able to discern an example of His Good Providence in
  the incident which happened to me one late winter day
as I was proceeding home from the mill with my team and a load of meal.

✦

This never-ending dream
of freedom and bread.

✦

I approached the river at a location where I had often crossed before, but,
being ignorant then of the devious and dangerous nature of the river and
  its ice at this time of the year,
I drove my oxen onto the river. When about half across, I perceived the ice
  settling under my animals.
I jumped onto the tongue of my sled and hastened to the oxen's heads and
  pulled out the pin that held the yoke.
By this time the oxen were sunk to their knees in water.
I then sprang to the sled and drawed it back to the shore without the least
  difficulty, notwithstanding the load, and returned to my oxen.

✦

I mean, in 1789 we *began* to arrive.
Not a steady stream, but waves—
like all migrations, conquerings, people driven from a place
by dissatisfactions, persecutions, restlessness, pulled toward
some other place by dream.

✦

By this time they had broken a considerable path in the ice and were
  struggling to get out.
I could do nothing but stand and see them swim round.
Sometimes they would be nearly out of sight, nothing scarcely but their
  horns to be seen;
they would then rise and struggle to extricate themselves from their perilous
  situation.

At length the oxen swam up to where I stood and laid their heads on the
  ice at my feet.
I immediately took the yoke from off their necks; they lay still till the act
  was performed
and then returned to swimming as before.

✦

First Anglo stock—English, Scot,
from the colonies to the south, mostly from Connecticut:
Stanton, Mead, Middlebrooks, Taylor, Lane, Sedgwick, Bacon,
Pettibone, Fairchilds, Kingsbury, Herrick, Crocker, Pixley, Shed.

And very shortly after, from the north,
maybe for the same reasons, the French came,
down across the border from Quebec:
Bourdeau, La Casse, La Croix, Ladeau, Larocque, Lavoie,
Le Blanc, Leroux, Levèsque, Poulin, Deschamps, Tétreault,
Desjardins, Devereaux, Patenaud, St. George, St. Jacques,
Turcotte, LaMotte, Bassette and Gelineau.

Again, later in the century, Italians, Spaniards, Greeks,
stonecutters come to work the quarries:
Scrizzi, Faziano, Albrizio, Tortellini, Gomez, Echeveria,
Rublacabla.

✦

By this time they had made an opening in the ice as much as two rods
  across.
One of them finally swam to the downstream side, and in an instant, as if
  lifted out of the water,
he was on his side on the ice, and got up and walked off;
the other swam to the same place and was out in the same manner.

I stood on the opposite side of the opening and saw with astonishment
  every movement.
I then thought, and the impression is still on my mind, that they were
  helped out by supernatural means; most certainly

no natural cause could produce an effect such as this;
that a heavy ox six and a half feet in girth, can of his own natural
  strength heave himself out of the water on his side on the ice.

✦

Then again, toward the end of the 1960s, another wave of young,
out of suburbs and cities and into these hills:
Hewitt, Landi, Klein, Liberman, Solomon, Plent.
Hippies.
Katzenberg, Bernstein, Coe.
Goddamned hippies!
All, pulled toward this place by dream.

✦

That in the course of Divine Providence events take place
out of the common course of nature that our strongest reasoning cannot
  comprehend
is impious to deny.
Others have a right to doubt my testimony, but in this instance, for me to
  doubt would be perjury to my own conscience
and ingratitude to my Divine Benefactor.

✦

Then in the 1970s yet another immigrant: coyote,
from the Dakotas, or Minnesota maybe, north to Canada
and east, where they mixed with timber wolves,
grew bigger, bushier, became "the new wolf,"
then dropped down again across the border.
Now their song is also added to this place.

It is fitting that this hybrid scavenger—want to call him bastard?—
should join us here, take up with us other illegitimates. Purity?
Source of madness, retardation, bane of Spanish kings.
Give me instead Thucydides Augustus McInnes
(he's known as Cyd).
Scot, Irish, Italian, who knows what else? Product of our mixing;

a foil, once, as we are now, to this hillbound, inbred, narrow
insularity. Some might call it madness. (I might call it that.)
Yet here we are, another wave, flowing toward tomorrow,
hybrids, immigrants, bastards: which is the way it's always been.

✦

When I reflect on past events, the fatigue and toil I had to endure, the
*   dark scenes I had to pass through,*
I am struck with wonder and astonishment at the fortitude and presence of
*   mind that I had then to bear me up under them.*
I exercised all my powers to the best I could, and left the effect for future
*   events to decide, without embarrassing my mind with imaginary evils.*
I could lie down at night, forgetting my troubles and sleep composed and
*   calm as a child.*
I did, in reality, experience the just proverb of the wise man,
that the sleep of the laboring man is sweet,
whether he eat little or much.

✦

Drawn toward this place by dream, we,
like those who came before, for reasons we can't speak,
take root, become this place, define it.

We are here and always leaving.
We are water, like the river,
just passing through.

✦

Nor can I close my tale of sufferings without rendering my feeble tribute of
*   thanks and praise to my Benign Benefactor,*
who supplies the wants of the needy and relieves the distressed, and who,
in His Providential Kindness has assisted my natural strength, both of
*   body and mind, to endure those scenes of distress and toil.*

✦

Providential Kindness, bless us,
and bless night-singing coyote.
Bless all souls alive in Judevine,
and bless the ghosts.

Give us Benediction.

✦ ✦ ✦

ROY MCINNES

I

Roy McInnes is a welder. He spends his life
with chains and block and tackle, steel and torches,
lives his days inside a hood looking like
a medieval warrior, peering through a small rectangle
of blackened glass, watching light brighter than the sun.
He listens to the groan of generators, the crack and snap
of an electric arc liquifying steel.
His hands are always dark and on his upper lip
is a mustache
as if wiped there by a greasy finger.

Roy McInnes is a small man and frail.
He speaks quietly and slowly and moves that way.
He seems at ease inside his body, comfortable there.
When you shake his hand his grip is warm and gentle
and you can feel the calm he carries in his person
flow into your arm.

Roy and I were visiting one day, years ago,
after we had got to know each other some,
and we got to talking about work
and I said, because I was afraid to tell the truth,
that I'd just about rather garden than do anything,
to which Roy responded, and there seemed to be
some sadness in his voice:
Well, I don't know about just about.
All I know is what I'd rather do than anything.
I'd rather weld.

II

Roy's truck is an extension of himself,
which is not to be confused with the way some people
buy a fancy car with velour seats, electric windows
and suddenly start wearing cardigans and oxfords,
suddenly become
little more than yet another piece of optional equipment.
In Roy's life it is the truck that gets transformed.

I met his truck the day I first met him.
Not that he introduced me or anything like that,
it's just you can't help noticing.

When Roy bought the truck new-to-him, it was just a pickup,
a common insect like a million others identical to it.
He brought it home, put it in his shop and six weeks later
it emerged a strange, metallic butterfly, unique and fanciful,
translated to
an articulation of his private vision,
a function of Roy's need and whimsy.

New, the truck was rated at three-quarter ton,
but with the added braces to the frame, heavier shocks,
special springs, dual rear wheels and heavy duty tires
it can carry four.

Roy cut the bed away right down to the frame
and welded on a diamond-plate floor and roof,
using two-inch steel pipe for posts, one at each corner,
one in the middle on each side. Then up forward,
toward the cab and halfway back, he welded
sheet-metal walls and welded sh elves to them
and all the shelves have doors on hinges, all made of steel.
There are hooks and clamps welded to the walls everywhere

so when he goes down a bumpy road his tools won't bounce
  around.

Roy McInnes is a carpenter who builds with steel,
with boilerplate and torches.
In place of nails he binds his dream
with hydrogen and oxyacetylene.

Shaper, molder, alchemist,
intermediary, priest,
his hands communicate a vision,
they create with skill and grace
an act of intercession between reality and need.

III

Roy's house and shop are on the edge of town.
The shop was built in stages.
The tall center section with its steep-pitched roof
is sided with slabs from the local mill, whereas
the lean-to shed on the left
is particleboard; the one on the right is Homasote.

Summer people say it's ugly, but what they can't, or won't,
understand is: the sidings write a history
of its construction. Rome wasn't built in a day either.

When Roy built the center section he needed an opening
large enough to admit big trucks, like loggers' rigs,
but couldn't afford the kind of rising, jointed,
overhead doors gas stations and garages have,
so he found a way to use salvaged storm doors,
the kind with glass so he could get some light in there,
by hitching them with hinges side to side
and stacking them three high so that now he's got

two folding doors which make an opening fifteen feet wide
and seventeen feet high: two doors of doors
made from eighteen smaller doors.

Roy heats the shop with a homemade, quadruple-chamber,
oil-drum stove: four fifty-five gallon drums:
two side by side above one, the firebox, and one above the two:
a glowing diamond of cylinders all welded to each other
and held apart by rods and all connected by a pipe
which leads the smoke from one drum to another and finally,
when it has bled the smoke of heat, exits to the chimney.

Beyond the stove at the back of the shop
stacked willy-nilly against the wall
there is an intricate confusion of iron pipes, cast iron scraps,
angle iron, sheets of aluminum and steel, diamond plate,
expanded metal, loops of heavy wire and braided cable
and a half-dozen categories of other things I can't identify—
a mine, the raw material of his dreams.

The shop is always cluttered, dirty, and there is
a permanent grime that clings to everything.
Generators and tanks of gas, and orange rubber hoses
snaked across the floor. The place smells of oil and grease,
of that molecular rearrangement of the air the welder's arc
produces.

This is a place where—against the grinder's scream and whine,
the moan of generators straining, the crackling spit of metal
rent asunder—human speech is pointless, drowned
in a cacophony of unearthly voices. And when the machines
get still, it is a place to see through the smoky fog
something medieval, brooding, dark, fantastical.

It would be so easy to see this place as sinister,

to see the wizard-priest who rules this lair as evil,
that would be so easy if
you didn't know that he is Roy—
the one who lets the calm of his body flow into your arm
when you touch his hand.

IV

Stand in the highway; look at the shop straight on;
pretend it isn't what it is; get beyond its function.
Look at its lines, at the proportions of height to width,
sheds to center section—an early Christian basilica,
or something Gothic.

The tall center section, narrow, steep-roofed—the nave.
The sheds—the aisles,
roofed-over flying buttresses.
And those doors of doors are cathedral doors.
There are no rose windows here, no clerestory, no triforium,
no vaulted ceilings or clustered piers, and it's ratty,
but it soars—not too high or very gracefully,
but it soars.

It is a January day.
The doors of doors fold open.
Roy appears in hood and grimy apron.

Then, just down the road, smoking through the village,
the penitent comes, the one who seeks the healing touch
of fire.

Guy Desjardins, trucker of logs and lumber,
who just this morning while loading the biggest butt-log beech
he ever saw in his life, snapped the boom.
The truck lurches down the road, clam and boom dangling,
a wounded beast, Gargantua's broken arm. Guy shifts down,

pulls to the doors of doors and in.

There are no acolytes, no choir,
but the engine sings its cracked and pulsing song
and the censer spurts heady clouds of smoke to the rafters.

The doors come closed, truck shuts down
and for a moment Guy and Roy stand
before the diamond juggernaut of cylinders, their hands
outstretched in ritualistic adulation, a prelude to the mass.
The boom is jacked and steadied, readied for the altar
of cutting flame: The Mass of Steel and Fire.

From the clutter of his accidental reredos
Roy brings angle iron. A ball-peen hammer bangs,
generator moans, light arcs and snaps, steel flows
a second time—a liquid balm, metallic salve
and the healing touch.

When the clanging mass is finished, when the groans
and snaps and spits have ceased, when there is silence,
when only a spirituous wisp of greasy smoke ascends
toward the blue-foggy rafters, when Guy stands
knowing it is done, the celebrant lifts his hood
and says benediction:
That ought to hold it, Guy.

They drink coffee from dirty cups,
eat doughnuts with greasy hands.
Then Guy backs out, is gone, smoking down the road,
back to the job, leaning on his horn and waving
in what has got to be plainsong, a canticle,
praise and joy for the man,
a chorus of hallelujahs, for
the reconciling arc of fire.

CYD

Thucydides Augustus McInnes went into the woods when he
   was twelve and spent his life logging with horses
and only at the age of eighty did he begin spending his winters in
   the welding shop with Roy, his son.

Yet even then he spent summers in the mountains, compromising
only in his last years by logging with a team of ponies because:
It got so I couldn't give the horses all the work they wanted.
I embarrassed them. These ponies here do less . . . like me.
We're suited to each other.

Thucydides Augustus McInnes was a logger for so long that there
are mountainsides around here he logged twice in his one lifetime.

When you met him, he did not reach out and shake your hand
as does his son, but rather he remained within himself
and bent his upper body forward, shyly. He almost bowed.

Thucydides Augustus McInnes was not a talker.
He could sit quietly not saying anything and visit—be—with you
and neither you nor he would be embarrassed.
It always seemed to me
he was a reincarnation of Lao Tzu.

Yet, lest you think him ephemeral or unearthly, he could dance,
even at the age of eighty, a clogging dance
with an authenticity, a verve and grace
no one who learns it for nostalgia's sake can ever muster.

The winter my wife carried our daughter in her womb,
Cyd came up with his ponies and his dray to help us draw our
   wood. I have a picture somewhere.
We are in the dooryard, at the woodshed door.

Snow is everywhere. We have just unloaded and have paused—
before we head back to the woods—
long enough for me to take the picture.
The ponies are waiting and steaming. My wife—my daughter
bulging beneath her coat—and Cyd stand on the empty dray.
Both of them are smiling. Cyd's cheek bulges with his plug,
you can see his stained tobacco teeth.
His eyes are warm and drenching—
alive as the sunlight on the first real day of spring.
His eyes are filled with his delight at being in the presence of this
beautiful and young woman who is carrying a child.

Thucydides Augustus McInnes, who was known as Cyd, and
    nobody's fool,
loved his horses and cared for them as well as any man. But—
and I must tell you this, because you should not get the wrong
    impression of this man, you should not think him soft—
I have seen him take his peavey and strike a horse on the hock
above a rear hoof and shout in fury at the beast until
the animal regained its understanding
of who it was gave the directions.

At the age of seventy-nine, Cyd went to Florida intending
to spend two weeks visiting with friends, but left two days
after his arrival and came home. When I saw him
down at The Garage and asked him how his trip had been,
he said: Well, sir, that place I was, that condominium,
had rules to keep out
all the animals and children.
Can you imagine that?
How could anybody spend his life without animals and children?

Thucydides Augustus McInnes died three days ago
and today was buried
up near the top of the sidehill cemetery just east of town,
the one that looks down—across the valley and the river,

97

the one that looks out—toward a mountainside
Thucydides Augustus McInnes
logged twice in his one lifetime.

SALLY TATRO'S PLACE

Even now, years after its desertion, and though it is
gray and sinking and its parts come apart, the house
still clings to a former grace—narrow clapboards,
fluted corners, a center door with frosted glass—
and, in addition to dishevelment, dilapidation,
the place suffers weeds high as the windows,
a porch roof fallen in, though it now
fades and weathers, slips irretrievably away,

when I drive past I watch and think how it is like
old poetry where reference and allusion are obscure
but where, even after centuries, insight and need
still swell within the form, and I see in the

collapsing house the builder's passion rising
from design: this indestructible, eternal dream.

ENVOY TO SALLY'S PLACE

There was a fellow passing through who lived and worked
in New York City, an official of some sort down there at the
Metropolitan Museum of Art is what I heard.
He was summering up here, I think, and going down the road
when he spied Sally's place and was so stunned
by its beauty and its calm, so taken aback by finding

such a work of art so far from anywhere,
he drove his car right off the road.

When Roy saw what happened he came running
figuring the fellow must be hurt, but before Roy could get
to where the car tilted in the ditch the fellow climbed out,
walked nonchalantly across the road
and began taking pictures of the house.

Roy comes up to him out of breath and says:
You okay?

And the gent turns around surprised and says:
Huh? Oh. Yes. Fine. Thank you.
and then says:
Does anybody here know how beautiful this place is?
Oh!

Roy didn't say much but did pull the fellow out
and he was on his way.

When Edith heard the story her mouth tightened as it does
when she gets mad and she said:
Yes, we know, or used to know.
It *was* a lovely place, but not now, not anymore.
What's beautiful about an empty house?
It's falling down, deserted, cold inside,
what's beautiful about that?

You should have seen that place when the Tatros
still were there, when there was flowers in the dooryard
and the barn wasn't falling down, paint on the clapboards
and wash on the line and the pastures clear because of cows—
then it was beautiful. Now it's just a wreck,
a picture for that fellow's old museum.

BEAUDRY'S LAWN SALE

A low-slung sagging house
those red-gray asphalt shingles
made to look like bricks
and the sheds of weathered wood
sagging too. All the roofs drooping.
Surrounded by ranks of gutted cars
and out front in the space
between the house and road
where there might have been
a lawn—a lawn sale instead.

Worn Formica kitchen tables,
the chrome legs blistering.
Coke and beer bottles, stacks
of plates and saucers (no two
alike), cups without handles,
electric motors that may
but probably won't work, one
overstuffed chair, six
television sets, old clothing,
innumerable knick-knacks and
everything covered with sheets
of plastic held down by rocks—
everything guaranteed dry.

This is a permanent sale.
Summer and winter it is here
which is why there is grass growing
in a cereal bowl or two.

If you are on the trail of an
antique, don't stop here—please.
This is not nostalgia's place.

No hidden gems resting unrecognized
amid the clutter. These people
know the worth of things
better than you think.

Here
are only bits and pieces
of a way of life,
these artifacts for sale:
the shards of want.

ELEGY FOR CHARLIE KETTER

I

Across the road from Beaudry's
was Charlie Ketter's—the nicest place in town.
His house and yard were always spic-and-span,
neat as a pin, and they therefore stood out
as a cared-for oasis
in the general rubble of the village.
He had a lawn, and the lawn was spread
with the wishing wells and birdhouses he made
and sold. His wishing wells were red and white
and blue and the birdhouses came in shapes
of sugarhouses, only you could never tell
which ones were for sale since he had a lot
of favorites that he never sold.

II

There was one thing odd about Charlie Ketter.
He was a Democrat, one of three in thirty-six
square miles. I heard a dozen people say:

I just can't understand that Charlie Ketter.
He's the nicest man what ever trod in shoes,
and he's a Democrat!

III

Charlie died two years ago
at the age of forty-three
of a cancer that daily
in the last year of his life
marched through his body
like hardhack and weed trees
filling in an unattended field.

IV

Now Charlie's wife is gone,
moved on to somewhere smaller,
and the Ketter place begins its turn
from order to decline, its fall
toward weeds and boards collapsed
upon themselves, a confusion
like a cancer
within the human frame.

JERRY'S GARAGE

In Craftsbury there are two: Raboin's and Humphrey's;
down in New Hampshire, in West Andover,
it is Thornley's;
in Five Islands, Maine,
it's called Grover's;
and between Lake Champlain
and the Atlantic Ocean there has got to be

a thousand known only as The Corner Store.

Almost all have gas pumps, only some
have mechanics or a post office
and I'd wager none
still have all three.

Here in Judevine we call it The Garage
or Jerry's.

Jerry's is
and is in
the center of the town.
It's not a place that used to be something else
and got converted to its present use. It's always been
a place for food and vehicles. First as a store and stable
and a wheelwright's shop, then, with cars, a store and gas pumps,
a mechanic and a lift. A place, since it began, to serve
two of the very few necessities: food and transportation.

The place that serves necessities becomes one;
which means, when there is nothing else to do,
when you are lonely, you go to The Garage
and stand around, or sit, and visit.

Conrad works at the garage because he may as well,
if he didn't have a job there he'd be there anyway,
which is why he got hired in the first place.
As Jerry smiling says: Hell,
if he's gonna be here all the time, he might as well
be doin' somethin'.

Conrad smirks and says: An' git paid.

Like all places of its kind

it's got a little bit of some things and not much of anything:
milk, eggs, lousy bread, tobacco—both to smoke and chew—
ammunition, candy, a smattering of canned goods,
toilet paper, a little dog food, one can of Similac,
fishing tackle, pickled eggs, produce when the season's right,
motor oil, the local papers, magazines,
maybe a book or two by a local writer, a little hardware,
and wine, shelves and shelves of wine and even more beer,
at least a couple coolers full—hundreds of cases
of beer.

For years Jerry talked about how he'd like to have
a restaurant hitched to the store—
there was an empty room out back would do.
It'd make it nice, he'd say, to have a place
to take a bowl of soup, a sandwich,
a place to sit and visit.
He talked that way for years,
then just a couple months ago
his dream got muscled out by deed
and Jerry's got himself a restaurant now—
a Judevine-type restaurant—
in the back room, the counter faced
in three different kinds of paneling,
a meat slicer he picked up at auction,
a hot plate from Alice's junk store and two
Formica kitchen tables and some chairs
with plastic seats from Beaudry's perennial lawn sale.

They make grinders, a different soup each day,
five days a week, and you can buy a soda in the store
to drink with lunch—but no beer,
unless you drink it outside,
the license costs too much.

Well, it ain't much. Jerry says:

Got some beat-up equipment, nailed together scraps.
(He's an ecologist, you see?)
Just like everything else in Judevine: half-assed.

Which it is and seedy too,
but such aesthetic judgments depend on point of view.
From where I look I see
something good enough for us or anybody:
a place to sit down, visit, eat and drink together,
even if it is a grinder and a Pepsi,
a place to let our caring for each other grow, which,
as everybody knows, has nothing at all to do
with soft lights and leather booths.

NEED, NECESSITY, DELIGHT,
OR,
A WASHING MACHINE FOR A FLOWERPOT

Every summer morning at fifteen minutes to seven
Jerry descends the stairs from his apartment above The Garage,
unlocks the store, turns off the nighttime lights,
turns on the gas pumps and the air compressor,
then moves to the lunchroom, plugs in the coffeepot
and, while he waits for his morning coffee,
he goes outside and wheels an ancient washing machine,
the kind that is a tub on legs, the legs on casters,
the wringer and the agitator long since gone,
away from the side of the building
and out to one end of the gas pumps.

The washing machine is full of dirt
and in the dirt grow giant orange and yellow marigolds.
He pinches off what blossoms may be dying, any withered leaves,
does the necessary weeding, and then, if they need it,

waters them with the battered, galvanized can
he uses to fill radiators.

In Jerry's old washing machine metaphored to flowerpot
I see the whole history of what I know of human art and thought.
Thales and Anaximander, thinking, trying to find that one thing
out of which all else comes, Pythagoras, slowly or
KA-BLAM! (as in Archimedes in the tub) when he discovers
a universal truth about certain kinds of triangles,
Anselm and Abelard as they debate the function of our words,
Hegel and the process of our thought,
or Einstein, fingers to his lower lip, dreaming
on the nature of time and space and energy.

Is it ridiculous to compare Jerry's flowerpot
to Einstein or Hegel, Abelard or Pythagoras?
They all took the old, the given, the known
and found in it something new,
that satisfying, exciting, delightful leap
of human sense and mind
from known to unknown.
Whether it is a washing machine for a flowerpot,
a pickup truck transmogrified to a specific need
or a poem
in which a ramshackled, tumbledown ratty pile of boards
known as a welding shop becomes a Gothic hymn to God,
it is the making of a metaphor, a bridge, that leap
from known to unknown.

To see the thing not for what it is or is thought to be
but for what it could be
because you must and must because
you are driven to delight by necessity, by need—
is imagination.

Some people look at Judevine and only see decay
because they don't remember necessity *or* need.
The words are lost somewhere inside them, pickled
in the sauce of affluence, atrophied by the tenure of security.
They don't remember that the decay they see is need
and need is the ground in which necessity
gives birth to the imagination.

When necessity gets pickled her child packs up and leaves,
goes some place else where she can find her mother.
Judevine is such a place.
Imagination lives here because her mamma lives here too.

In the midst of what some think is squalor,
necessity and the imagination yield delight—
like Roy's truck and shop, or Jerry's flowerpot,
these metaphors,
for the eternal, elemental searching of the human soul—
and they bloom,
because this ground is rich with need.

BEN

You can see him in the village almost anytime.
He's always on the street.
At noon he ambles down to Jerry's
in case a trucker who's stopped by for lunch
might feel like buying him a sandwich.
Don't misunderstand, Ben's not starving;
he's there each noon because he's sociable,
not because he's hungry.
He is a friend to everyone except the haughty.

There are at least half a dozen families in the village

who make sure he always has enough to eat
and there are places
where he's welcome to come in and spend the night.

Ben is a cynic in the Greek and philosophic sense,
one who gives his life to simplicity
seeking only the necessities
so he can spend his days
in the presence of his dreams.

Ben is a vision of another way,
the vessel in this place for
ancient Christian mystic, Buddhist recluse, Taoist hermit.
Chuang Tzu, The Abbot Moses, Meister Eckhart,
Khamtul Rimpoche, Thomas Merton—
all these and all the others live in Ben, because

in America only a dog
can spend his days
on the street or by the river
in quiet contemplation
and be fed.

CONRAD

Conrad. Forty-three.
Works at The Garage
rents a room from Flossie
just next door
has his separate entrance so
everything will be
on the up-and-up.

Changes tires, takes the bottles
but never works the register.

What do I owe you, Conrad?
Well . . . you . . . I don't know.
You better go ask Jerry.

Every evening when the valley darkens
just about the time
the lights go on above the gas pumps,
Conrad begins. Beer
and blackberry brandy.
By closing time at eight
he hovers in the low and darkened room
like a dazed cat.

Jerry locks up, puts out the lights,
except for the one in the window that says:

Beer

and Conrad pads the hundred feet to home
tilting between
broken cars and snow machines,
headed for his separate entrance.

Supper? Huh?

The beer is filling.
Think of all those calories.
The sugar in the brandy
gives him carbohydrates.
His protein comes from television.
He dines each night in black and white.
He builds his bone and muscle from
a two-dimensional dream.

Now he is rugged, handsome, swift and mean.
There is a gorgeous woman hanging on his sleeve.

Conrad's only failure is as a novelist.
He never learned to lie. Don't pity him.
Pity yourself instead. Ask if you have more
or whether it is simply, as it is with me,
that you write better fiction for your life.

JERRY WILLEY'S LUNCH

Before Jerry got The Garage he worked for the Mountain
 Company down in Stowe
helping New York ladies off the lifts,
all day on top the mountain freezing his ass off
for two and a quarter an hour.
Jerry never brought a lunch, not once in all those years,
just six pieces of bread, a jar of mayonnaise and a soda which
each morning when he reached the mountain top he placed
inside the warming hut beside the skiers' lunches
left there so they wouldn't freeze.

As Jerry said: I ain't eatin' salt pork and macaroni
when I got these. Then he'd unwrap half a dozen
skiers' sandwiches, extract a slice or two from each—
roast beef, corned beef, ham, pastrami—
rewrap them carefully and fix his lunch.

THE GASTRONOMIC TRIPTYCH
WHICH IS SAM HINES' LIFE

Sam Hines divides his life like most of us
by years
but unlike most of us
he breaks each year
into three parts
not four or twelve.
Seasons and months mean nothing to him.
He never knows what time it is,
what day or week;
he only knows the time by what he eats.

When I feel the sun get higher in the sky
I begin to dream 'bout sugarin'
an' when we boil that first time
I go onto maple syrup right away
an' hit it hard
an' stay with it until it's time for trout.
Then I stay with them until the frost comes
an' leaves come down an' I get the itch
to kill a deer. When I've got me one,
I stay with him right through the snow 'n dark;
only I can't hit him hard the way I do the trout 'cause
he's got to last me 'til the sun gets back up here
an' I can go again onto the syrup.

Works good. Except those years I don't kill a deer.
Those are hard winters an' I'm use'ly always sick,
an' sometimes I'm so sick
I think I'll die an' never make it to the syrup.
But I always have, by Jesus—
only sometimes, Mister Man,
it's been awful close.

LUCY AND JERRY

I first met Lucy where everybody meets her
at Jerry's Garage
which is the only place she ever goes.

We hadn't lived here long when one day she got me cornered
back by the coolers:

What's your name? We've got the place, the last one,
just on the edge of town. You know the place?
House is on the right, barn's just across the road.
You ought to stop in sometime; we'll show you around.
We got a nice place. We're all Jerseys you know.
It's just the three of us, my husband and my son and me,
nobody else. We do it all ourselves.
Only don't come today. My husband and my son
aren't home right now, but they'll be coming back—
maybe tomorrow.
My son's in the war you know. In the navy,
the only one from here what joined the navy.
He's on a battleship. He sends us letters almost every day
all about how hot it is, says it's not at all like here.
My husband always wanted to be a sailor,
but he was farming when the war broke out
so they wouldn't let him go.
We been on our place since nineteen and thirty-five.
Jerseys you know. We never have anything but Jerseys.
You married? Bring your wife and kids.
We'll show you around. Only don't come today.
Come by tomorrow—I think they'll be back by then.
I got to go. Stop by. They could be back anytime.
We'll show you around, only not today. Come by tomorrow.

When I paid for my beer, Jerry didn't say a word about the
    woman. He acted as if what she said

112

wasn't at all unusual. The second time I saw Lucy
she launched into the same thing again almost word for word
and again Jerry didn't say anything about it.

Then slowly, over the years,
I heard about her and little by little
the pieces converged until I had her story.

Their son graduated high school in 1942 and within a month
had joined the navy, been shipped out to the South Pacific.
He boasted all over town before he left that he'd:
Take care of them Japs and be home by Christmas.

That was two years before they got the news.
It was August 1944, haying was just done
when they received the letter.
He had been their only child.

All the husband said that anybody can remember was:
Well, I guess some Jap took care of him instead.

The neighbors called, brought food.
Lucy and her husband accepted all the overtures, but they
neither smiled nor cried nor offered any thank-you.

About a week after they received the news
Lucy's husband hung himself in the barn one morning
after chores. Lucy has been living alone in the house
since then.

Jerry told me once that he used to try to explain to strangers,
after she had left, just how she was, but he gave it up because
it was too difficult and besides, although he never told me this,
I think he discovered somewhere along the way
that he knew and cared for Lucy more than any stranger, and thus
he became an accomplice to her dream, a role to this day

he knowingly and gladly plays.

It used to be she'd talk to anyone who'd listen.
She told everyone over and over again,
how her husband and her son were coming home,
maybe tomorrow,
until it became obvious, even to her, she couldn't go on
doing that. Since then,
she has spoken only to strangers who haven't heard her story.

But Lucy is growing older, she's sixty-nine now, and it's become
difficult for her to remember who is stranger and who is not
and who might be a little bit of both, which is the cause
of the incident that happened just the other day.

There's a youngish man in town who's been around awhile.
He was in the store when she came in and she, not remembering
that he'd heard her dream before, began again.
When she was maybe halfway through the youngish man
exploded:

You're crazy, old woman! You're crazy!
I've heard that story half a dozen times.
They're never coming back! Never!
Somebody ought to put you in the loony bin!

And Lucy was saying:
No. No.
It's true. It's true. Really, it's true.

and:

They're coming home. Maybe even tomorrow.

As she spoke, Jerry, who is not a big man,
came out from behind the counter and seized the youngish man
around the neck the way wrestlers do

and the man's face turned red then blue.
Jerry drug him out the door
and threw him down to the ground beside the gas pumps
and only then did Jerry speak and say:
Mister, don't you ever come in here again.

Then Jerry came inside and stood with his hands
spread out on the counter and he was breathing hard and shaking.
Jerry looked up at me then turned his face toward Lucy
who was standing calmly now at the counter with her groceries
and her money. Then in more years than anyone can remember
she spoke to someone she knew and said:

Jerry, you sure get some crazy people in here.

✦ ✦ ✦

BETWEEN HILLS BRIEFLY GREEN

I

If you want me, you know where to come.
Any Tuesday night or Sunday afternoon,
I'll be there, slapping hot ones through the box,
liners up the middle, out at second in my crouch
and pounding on my glove, waiting for that sizzler
from the lady with the harp and wings—
the one to whom I say and sing,

> *Come on, Baby, Come on*
> *put it down here if you dare.*
> *I got fast hands, and soft hands too, and*
> *I can take your shots.*
> *You ain't got much can make it past me into right.*

And then I sing to her and say,

> *I'm a softballer, Baby, and*
> *   I know how to play the game.*
> *I said, I am a softballer, Baby,*
> *   and I do know how to play the game.*
> *Why don't you come some night and watch me, Honey,*
> *   I just know you'll be awful glad you came.*
> *   (I said, I know you will be glad you came.)*

II

You've got to understand: here winter stays six months a year—
I mean snow, cold, ice, slush, high wind
out of the north and west.
Thirty, forty below, but raw and ugly at thirty-five above too.
Mean, mean winters and too long, six months too long.

Ninety days of frost-free weather is what we get,

and in those ninety days we cram a year's supply
of vegetables, barbecues, a thousand thousand tons of hay,
mowers across the lawn, apples, a litter of pigs,
the drive-in movies, afternoons swimming in a pond,
a new shed, dances out-of-doors,
the fair, sun tans, sex with warm feet, and softball.

From all over town we come: out of the winter dead:
LeRiche, LeCoss, LeMare, LaMarche, Dubois, Harris,
Richardson, Budbill, Putvain, Ward, Tallman, Reed,
Scrizzi, Gomez, Rublacabla, Antonioni, Smith, Cochran,
Willey, Kenniston, Klein, Albrizio, Westover, Manning
and Bourdeau.

Out of cold and dark to be in the sun, under the blue sky,
between hills briefly green, to play on a mown field, to
run and jump and field and throw, to hit the ball and holler:
to play softball.

III

Leave the village going west, pass the Dunn Hill road and take
the hard right just beyond where the blue-and-white sign wired
to a snow-fence post proclaims:

Ballfield
and
Gravel Pit

and an arrow pointing up the road.

Up through the gulf where it is always dark,
where hemlocks lean and bow—
half a mile up through to where the road bends right
and where the left bank is cut away for sand, to where
Robert's backhoe, name of Drott, sits under the leaning cliff,

to where another sign, in blue and white, announces:

Ballfield
contact Henry Mead
or call: 888-3729
for sand and gravel too.

Turn left. Enter slowly and shift down.
Climb the knobby ruckled way to Henry's
Gravel Pit and Ballfield.

Twist the switchback to the first plateau,
drop down into the used up pit, weave
across the sandy track past low bushes
struggling through stones, this gray-barren
canyon, dry and dusty, cross section of
the body we walk upon, here in Vermont.

Then up the final climb to grassy flat
level as a skillet, billiard table, softball field—
green skin over this glacial dump, a treasure trove,
two hundred feet of stones and sand ten acres round.

Tuesday nights we practice, a pickup game amongst ourselves
until it's dark. On Sunday afternoons we play doubleheaders
in a league.

IV

Tuesday, 6:00 P.M. The cars and trucks are just now pulling in.
Leo and Robert in Robert's pickup and I leaning on the door.
Leo: Couldn't sleep at all last night or the night before.
Robert: How's that?
Too excited. Laid awake all night hittin' those two homers
I hit Sunday over and over again.

And in my dream which is my fantasy this is what I see:

118

It is the third batter of the inning, men on first and second, there
because of me, the grounders I let through my legs.
I'm playing second. The batter is left-handed. I'm pulled over
more than half the way to first.

He sends a searing, screaming liner
(the man on second is already gone)
over the pitcher's head, headed directly for the gap in center.

I scramble to my right and leap and soar eight feet
into the air above the bag. I spear the ball backhanded and I drop
like an eagle landing onto second doubling the runner
who by now is half the way to third.
I turn, seize the ball bare-handed and race
toward first, toward that befuddled, turning runner, and I
gently touch him with the ball. Then loose-boned and cool
I flick the ball toward the pitcher's mound and shamble
toward the bench where my mates are standing
dumbfounded, incredulous at my unassisted triple play.

V

So we pass the summer and when the air cools and everybody
every night covers their tomatoes, when you can stand
at home plate and see across the valley on the hills
the popple and red maple turning yellow, red . . .

we give up this game, go home, put our gloves away and begin
that long slide toward another winter.
And we miss each other,
miss those Tuesday nights and Sunday afternoons.

Now separate, insular, wrapped in cold and dark, we—like our
gloves wrapped and lying on the closet floor—wait
for our summer lives, wait until again spring says
peas and spinach and softball. We wait for the game,

for that diversion which is so much better than to work
because it is to play, because it is to laugh and sweat
and not to care at all or even think
about tomorrow.

✦ ✦ ✦

THE MILL

I

Beside the brook, below the road, just down from Jerry's
and just above the river, the old gristmill stands,
by far the biggest building in town, plain and solid,
quiet, functional, not a single frill,
its narrow clapboards weathered gray,
and at the corners their horizontal lines abut
the vertical soar of column, New England's
wooden imitation of Doric simplicity.
This elegant box with steep-pitched gabled roof of slate,
broad eaves, three feet of overhang, the corner soffits
open in the old style, a delight to phoebes.
These granite stairs enduring through an age of use
that lead to loading dock and door, worn to a sag—
a hundred years, how many tons?—of grain and people in,
flour and people out. The wheel is gone as is the grain
but the stone millrace remains, and this place remains,
whole but mute, vestige of another age.
Once a necessity, now it hunkers at the junction
of brook and river, witness to an imagined time
of order and design, its nine eyes opening
toward a world irrevocably changed.

II

On the gabled end, toward the road, the building has
nine openings, eight windows and a door.
When taken together into the eye these openings
become the annotations to a score
which sings of other days.
Nine openings ordered in four rows.
The first: a center door, a window to each side
    all equidistant from each other
      and from the Doric corners.

the second: three windows, a perfect repetition of the first,
    notes in unison, although the center window
    is larger than the rest because it is also
    an upper door and because it is the precise center
    of the building and the song.
the third: two windows placed to syncopate
    the now established beat, yet these too
    positioned equidistant from each other
    and from the corners.
the fourth: a single window singing simultaneously
    both unison and syncopation, syncopation
    to the windows of the third floor, in unison
    with the center window of the second floor
    and with the first floor door—
the fourth: a single window, culmination, coda,
    a soaring to the eaves,
    to ridge and peak,

    to where the eye leaps
    into the village-valley air and sees
    these wooded hills.

ALICE TWISS

I

The mill is Alice Twiss' junk store now.
Four stories high and filled to the top,
each floor, each enormous room glutted, crammed,
pressed full, mounded to the ceiling with everything
anyone could ever pick up and carry away.
And narrow passages leading here and there
through the dark. In all of humanity only Alice
knows what's there and where it is,
and the place so full

the things spill out into the sun
between the building and the road, beside the brook,
behind, along the river, old drays, sledges, sleighs,
Coca-Cola coolers, a display case from a butcher shop,
a couple of Fairbanks scales, an iron wheel John Deere,
washing machines, some freezers and
a 1947 Packard without a hood.

When her pickup's there she is too and waiting
just inside the door on a stool in the faint light
of a window that hasn't been washed in a hundred years.

She: Alice: the Minotaur, returned, this time friendly,
creator, keeper, guide to the Labyrinth of Judevine
(mythology forever repeats itself but never exactly)
this time not half-bull, half-man but
half-woman, half-man, as you will see.

I pull my pickup off the road and stride toward the mill.
For a moment I am Theseus. I will wander down the Labyrinth
unraveling a ball of string and when I find the beast
I will slay it, follow the yarn back to the light of day,
back to my Ariadne, back to Athens
where I will assume the throne
and having assumed it
abandon it and create
de-moc-ra-cy!

Nah.

This is another time and I don't like such fantasies.
What's here is good enough. What I want to say is what I see.
This is not Epidaurus, nor am I the prince.
Besides, you don't need string. Alice has a flashlight.

I mount the granite steps.

Hi, Alice.

Hi.

I'm looking for a handful of three-eighths-inch,
fine-thread, reverse-turn bolts.

Yuh.

She rises, turns on a flashlight whose batteries are
almost dead and follows the yellow glimmer
down passages so narrow sometimes the searchers
must move sideways, stoop and duck, passages more like
tunnels, vague shapes looming on all sides,
dangling overhead, lost in gloom.

Then turning in the chill she stops,
reaches through the murk, extracts,
from a heap of chairs, snowshoes, old tables, electric motors,
overcoats, hammerheads and axe handles, a rusted metal box
and out of it she takes a handful of
three-eighths-inch,
fine-thread, reverse-turn
bolts.

Two dollars.

At the door again, I pay her. She wears a rubber thumb guard
for counting money, like the one my father wore, when he drove
a streetcar, for counting transfers, and with business done
her taciturnity dissolves and we have a visit.

II

Been fishin' lately, Alice?

I was out at daylight just this morning
up on Pond Brook,
but I only got enough for breakfast.

Usually you do better than that.

Usually I get my limit.
But that Sam Hines has got that brook cleaned out.

He doesn't.

He does!
He don't stop when it's time to quit, ya know.
You know he takes too many.

You don't do too bad yourself, Alice.

But I stay within my limit.
It ain't right the way he does.

III

You don't want to deal with Alice unless you know
exactly what you want and what you want to pay.
She deals hard and won't dicker. She'd rather
take that place with her to the grave than imagine
she'd been taken. There was once though,
in anybody's memory—
no doubt the time she learned her lesson—
when she was bested,
and by Hermie Newcome too.

It happened years ago, so I don't know for sure
if what they say is true. One day Hermie came down
off the hill wanting for a stone boat, and offered Alice
a dollar for the hood to the Packard. She took it and

the Packard's been there ever since, unwanted.

Some people say Hermie got the best of her that day
because he'd had the best of her before
but that could not be true.

IV

Alice is five one or two,
mouse brown hair, kept short, combed back
in what was known once as a ducktail,
but her hair is always clean, as she is, even though
she has a dirty job. She wears pants and shirts,
pullover sweaters, sometimes a sports coat,
corduroy or tweed, shoes and boots from L. L. Bean.

Like many women in these parts she loves to hunt and fish.
Her pickup has a camper on the back
and in the rear window a gun rack from which she hangs,
depending on the season, a shotgun, a .30-30 or a fishing pole.
She catches more trout than Sam Hines and between them
every summer there is a not-so-private competition.
Alice has won Jerry's buck pool more than any man in town.

Alice also has a bike, a Harley-Davidson, which she rides
to work each day the weather's good.
She keeps the bike as clean as she keeps herself,
wheels free of mud, chrome gleaming.
The bike has saddlebags, the rigid kind,
and rearview mirrors looming above the handlebars.
From each mirror flows a raccoon's tail
off animals she shot herself.
Alice claims she's had the thing up to a hundred and twenty.

I believe her.

Although Alice deals hard and won't dicker,
once you get to know her you can tell her what you want
and she will dig for it, bring it around and be fair
about the price.

Alice is the best to visit with, a storyteller
and a talker. She does what most people never think
to do, she asks you about yourself, how your work is going,
what you've been up to. Alice embraces other people's lives.

I love Alice.
Unlike visiting with a man, I never feel, when I'm with her,
that little twang of competition. And unlike visiting
with a woman, I never feel the discomforting, exciting
dance of sexuality, the aching in the fingertips.

Being with Alice is undistracted relaxation,
unmitigated pleasure in the presence of another being,
whom I can love, and she love me, no strings attached.

I know this simple, crippled joy
with no other human in this world.

ENVOY TO ALICE

I was down to Jerry's not long ago
and Alice was there which is not unusual
since it's where she goes to warm herself
in the winter when the mill's too cold
to stand the place for long.

There was a woman with her,
older than Alice and slight, but taller.
She wore a dress.

I said hello, paid for my things
and left, aware
of an unwanted, disconcerting jealousy.

✦ ✦ ✦

ABRAHAM WASHINGTON DAVIS

I

A colonel in the Vermont Regiment brought him north
to Burlington after the Civil War and named him
Abraham Washington Davis. Davis was fifteen then
and couldn't read a word. Eight years later
he graduated from the university first in his class—
an educated, liberated slave. He read Latin, Greek,
knew the classics. After graduation
he worked as a schoolmaster over the hill from here
in Craftsbury. Then in 1875 he came to Judevine
to organize the church.

He was the only black man for fifty miles around
and must have been a curiosity. Black people still are
in this white place.

In 1877 he married Dora Glenn, a local girl.
They had a little farm up behind the church.

A month or so after they were married Dora died in childbirth,
the baby too. The two of them are buried side by side
in the cemetery by the church but nobody can remember now
which grave is theirs, not even Laura Cate who knows more
about the cemeteries in this town than anyone alive.

Davis left not long after his wife and baby died
and nobody ever heard from him again.

There's a story goes around though that he never left Vermont,
that he lived like a hermit in a shack, without any books,
up near Island Pond. People up that way, they say,
didn't even know he could read.

Edith claims that when he died the folks in Craftsbury

brought the body back to the Academy. She knows because
when she attended high school there in the nineteen-twenties
it was his skeleton which hung from a metal pole
in the biology room. She knows, she says, because
it was a Negro's skull.

II

One of the ways we pass the time up here
is in that peculiar form of conversation
known as "visiting." There is never a topic for the talk
and no one talks about what they've read or seen on the TV
and almost no one ever offers an opinion or says
what he or she thinks
unless it is to voice a cliché about the government or welfare
or to say what they think about somebody; rather,
the words come out as stories from the past,
jokes and tales about people and events
(which is why I write the way I do)
and in this form there are ritualistic phrases
which repeat themselves, as when Hiram
refers to eating sponge cake as
"like walking through a thick fog with your mouth open";
or there are phrases applied to attitudes or people such as
"burled up like a cat who's seen a fox,"
"glad of spring as a phoebe in the sugarhouse,"
"plain as a hare in a December without snow,"
"fits like a glove on a rooster's foot,"
"cold as a white blackbird with four buckle galoshes,"
"dumb as a frog,"
"strong smelling as an old buck nigger."

When that last phrase rises and hangs in the air
I am transported
and I see Dora Glenn and the infant stir in their graves.
I see the biology room, the skeleton and the pole
and slowly, while I watch, the bones take flesh and form,

130

his body reemerges. He is fully clothed, a suit and vest,
high starched collar above wide tie,
his intelligent, gentle face,
the thin mustache, the short-cropped, tight-dark hair;
lover, father, scholar, teacher, priest:
vision of dignity—suspended from a pole.

I remember one time—no, many times,
while working in the woods when things were tough and ugly
and somebody'd say: This ain't no work for a white man.
We need a couple niggers.

Abraham Washington Davis suspended from a pole . . .
twists and turns,
rotates in the air—

a dark man
in our dark.

✦

The story about Abraham Washington Davis' skeleton being in
    the biology room isn't true.
I found the truth years after I had heard the story.
He did not retreat into his grief and live alone as a hermit up in
    Island Pond;
he left Vermont and went out to Ohio where he spent his life
    teaching at an all-black college there.
He taught Greek and Latin, the classics of the white man's
    literature from Homer to Virgil.
He remarried, had four children, died, and is buried in
    Wilberforce, Ohio.

Why this story about his skeleton had currency in these parts is
    not a mystery.
It is commentary on the racism all us white folks carry with us to
    this day.

FLOSSIE

There will be a crowd.
The dinner is famous.
Flossie can lose herself in folks
who come in station wagons,
bring the kids; she can
slip in, fill herself and go.
The paper said donation.
The people at the church will turn the other way.

She wears a blue bright dress with yellow flowers,
a circus tent for her
elliptical body.

She tilts down the highway like a metronome.
Her mop handle staff beats time.
Her strand of pop pearls knows
the tempo.

Now with a hundred others in the basement of the church,
Flossie doesn't smile, doesn't say hello.
She eats.

Two bowls of oyster stew.
The spoon's too small.
She puts it down; finds another, larger,
next to someone else's plate.

She scoops the oysters out.
She lifts the bowl and drinks.

Two plates of casseroles.
The big spoon still
is best.
Her eyes follow the spoon, her palsied hand,

like cats watching a bird.

The spoon moves around her plate
filling itself with food.
It flutters to her mouth.

Sweat gathers between her eyebrows, slips down
her nose and falls at intervals
on baked beans and macaroni salad.

She sees nothing but her spoon
filling itself with food.

She tilts her plate, not with fingers
but a quaking fist, scoops the juice,
goes for pie, for cake
and coffee, three cups
with lots of cream and sugar.

She puts a couple biscuits in her purse,
meets her staff at the door,
is gone.

Flossie tilts and belches down the road.
Back to the silent house, back to
cat piss in the woodwork.

The bright blue ellipsis, the metronome,
tilts down the road.
The staff beats time.
The necklace sways.

TWELVE OLD LADIES ALL IN BLACK

Twelve old ladies all in black,
wards of the state, farmed out up here,

in the enormous ancient paintless house
in which Philemon Wood once lived,
just on the edge of town,

every morning walk
a great big circle single file
around the pasture beside the house

and watch their feet as each one moves
around, around this groove in earth,
this ring of exercise, this circle
which is not a wholeness,

and some of them may be conversing
with themselves as they turn 'round
this ring for the forgotten,

and all of them, their heads cast down,
their lives thrust inward, burn

upon the pyre of remembering.

✦ ✦ ✦

THE POSTMASTER AND THE CLERK

I

Every morning at exactly six
Edgar Whitcom rises.
He bathes in a basin at the kitchen sink—
his face and hands, his arms,
chest and stomach—down to his waist.
He dries himself and hangs the basin back
on a hook above the sink beside the window
which looks out on the river which is
running,
running away.

Then he fills a glass with water, drops his toothbrush in
and shakes a small amount of dental powder
onto the palm of his left hand.
Edgar Whitcom is sixty-one years old. He has yet
to buy a tube of toothpaste.
He scrubs his teeth and watches out the window toward the river
which is moving, restless, always new,
and running,
running away.

He shaved with an electric razor before retiring last night—
so as not to intrude upon the stillness of this morning
or disturb his anticipation of the day to come.
He boils an egg, boils water for his tea, and cuts
a slice of bread from a loaf Laura Cate has made for him.

Breakfast ready, he moves it to the sink
and takes it slowly, standing at the window
in the company of the river,
muddy, dark, unknown,

running,
running away.

He dons his undershirt and shirt,
a white shirt, clean and fresh,
as each is,
six working days a week.
He ties a perfect four-in-hand knot in his tie,
without looking, while
looking out the window toward
the swollen, swelling river which is
running,
running away.

Throughout these daily matins
Edgar Whitcom neither sings nor hums
but moves lightly through the silent house
wrapped in his anticipation. And,
like a contrapuntal melody to his eagerness,
he hears another song and knows
the still comfort of the known,
his egg and tea, the bread, his shirt,
the window and the river.

Now he prepares a lunch,
a sandwich and a piece of fruit,
puts it in a paper bag, pours what tea is left
into a thermos, puts on his coat and hat,
both of which he brushed last night,
steps out the door and walks eastward leisurely
the two hundred yards to the post office here in Judevine.

He unlocks the door, begins another day
as postmaster to this town, something he has done
each working day for the past thirty-seven years.

He removes his coat and hat and, pushing his chin
hard into his neck, straightens the tiny ceramic pin
on his left lapel which says:

U.S. Postal Service
Thirty Years

He combs his hair, unlocks the safe,
then stands at his desk and watches through the window
toward the mercurial river,
dark and violent,
limpid, lurid, still
by turns.

At exactly nine each morning
Edgar Whitcom leaves what he is doing
and without his coat or hat strides
to the town offices just next door.

Laura Cate looks up and smiles
and Edgar Whitcom says: Good Morning!
and she replies: Hello!
They visit about the weather, how they are feeling,
anything that comes to mind,
and as they do they look
deeply and directly
into each other's eyes.

Edgar Whitcom eats at noon, but before he sits down at his desk
with his paper bag and thermos
he pulls up a second chair and presently
Laura Cate comes through the door, lunch in hand,
and they take their meal together.

Sometimes they visit while they eat,
and sometimes Edgar Whitcom's laughter fills the room

and Laura Cate feels as if the sound of his voice
is dark and furious water bearing her away to places
she has never been. And Edgar Whitcom too,
when he sees her face, hears her voice,
feels the anticipation that enveloped him that morning
flow away like water. He too is borne away
on the rocking current of her voice.
He feels himself unfold and rise
like the river when it swells.

Other times they take their meal in silence
watching together out the window
toward the immodest, intemperate river
which is running,
running away.

II

Every morning at exactly six,
Laura Cate also rises.
She removes her sleeping clothes, bathes herself,
puts on a dress, or a skirt and blouse, depending on her mood
(she has never in her life worn a pair of pants),
puts on her shoes, which match the morning's clothing,
applies lipstick sparingly, pats powder to her face and daubs
perfume behind each ear.
She combs her hair, smooths out the wrinkles in her clothing,
then moves to her kitchen where she prepares her breakfast.

Laura Cate is fifty-two, big-boned and stately,
an unseen beauty in an age of bony women.

When she's prepared her breakfast, she takes it to the table
in her tiny dining room and as she eats
she watches through the window
to the swollen, churning river.

With breakfast done, her lunch packed,
she returns to the tiny dining room and sits at the table
with her last bit of coffee in the presence
of the morning light and of this
restless, moving river which is
running,
running away.

Then she rises, puts on her coat, hangs her purse
from the crook of her folded arm, puts her cup and saucer
in the sink and leaves her house, and as she does she sings:

> *You are my sunshine, my only sunshine.*
> *You make me hap-py when skies are gray.*

She walks down the short path to the road, turns westward
and steps off intently toward the town clerk's office
three hundred yards away.

For twenty-five years she has been clerk to the town of Judevine;
twenty-five years the arbiter of documents,
the keeper and preserver of all legalities.

When the office is ready for the day's transactions,
and her day's work lies before her on the desk,
she moves to the window and with her arms
folded beneath her breasts, Laura Cate watches out the window
toward the river, the lucid, energetic river
as it runs,
runs away.

At five minutes to nine Laura Cate removes her lipstick
and her compact from her purse and touches up her mouth,
powders her nose, looks carefully at herself in the compact's
tiny mirror. Then she waits to hear: Good Morning!
Waits to say: Hello!

III

Late every winter in a narrow tray at the United States Post Office
in Judevine, Vermont, Edgar Whitcom grows the seedlings
of pansies and calendula.
In the town offices just next door in another tray
Laura Cate grows marigolds and cosmos.

When spring comes, Laura Cate and Edgar Whitcom
meet each other at the flower bed between the doors
to till the soil and plant their flowers.

Sometimes on a summer morning you can see them there
weeding between the plants, pinching off the dying blossoms
and you can hear them talking, laughing with each other.

IV

Every Sunday Laura Cate walks down the road to church.
Edgar Whitcom waits inside his house and watches.
When the time is right, he strides out the door,
across the road and meets her,
whereupon she takes his arm
and they enter church together.

When the benediction has been said, they leave the church
and take their Sunday meal together,
then together walk beside the river,

the roiled and swollen, muddy, violent river,
the lucid, easy, quiet river,
this river,
their blood,
their passion and delight,
that for thirty years has moved
through their lives,

always changing, always new,
running,
while they watch and stay,
these two who watch and stay,
companions to each other, to the river
while the river runs away.

ANTOINE ON THE BOWSER FACTORY, FREE ENTERPRISE, WOMEN, LOVE AND LONELINESS

David, you got pair of tweezer?

Huh?

I got to take a pee!
Ah, never min'. I'll find it.

Pardon me, David, if you would please.
I'm gonna to turn my back on you, so you can't see
my little wimen's biggest disappoin'ment!

Ah, David, I'm gettin' sick of dis.
I can't stand it too much longer.
We got to open dat bowser factoree like we talk about.
Make dem pussy wigs for da wimens.
Red one, yellow one, black kinky one,
red-white-an'-blue one for da pa'tri'its. . . .
Dat be da t'ing!

In dis country, David, you can't get ahead workin' out like dis.
You got to go it on your own, haf' saum 'magination,
be da boss, not just another sla'f like we be here day after day.

You and me, David, we put our money all tagedder
open up dat factoree.
We go 'raound fraum door to door, sell dem wigs,
tell da wimens: Hey, it be da latest t'ing. And . . .
we be da fidders too, you and me!
Saum job!

First place we go
be to dat hippie girl live up da road from our place.
Why,
she be saumt'ing like you never see!

Ow! Saints in da trees! What we do widout da wimens!
Dis life ain't built for to live it all alone.
I be forty-five, dat half a ninety, what I'll never see,
before I find my wimens. An' all dem years I'm livin' to myself
in dat tin can with naut'in' but my goddamn dog.
We ain't built for to live dat way.
You got to have somebody be wid', saumbody talk to, cry wid',
roll around da bed, sid across da table from.
You can't live touchin' nat'in' but a goddamn dog.

Da Lord he make plenty mistake when he build dis place an' us
is what I t'ink, only you don't tell da priest I say so,
but one t'ing he got right was when he made da wimens.
David, you know what I mean—how your han' ache to hold her.
Dey be so different fraum da likes a us.
Like my cat an' dog what loves each odder an' don't fight
only cuddle up and lick each odder all da time.

Wimens is good for da pecker an' da soul,
and, Mister, you get 'em bod 'n one an'
you got saumt'in' better dan da world!

Aow! All dis talkin' make me itch to see her,

haf' saum tea an' touch'er face.
So why I be here wid you all da afternoon?
Good-bye. I see you!

✦ ✦ ✦

THE HOPPER PLACE

Down Creamery Street
just across the tracks
there's a burnt-out cellar hole
full of rusting junk and charred remains—
what's left of where the Hoppers used to be.
They're in a shack now, up on the bank
behind the ruin. There's the Hopper woman,
two of her men, six kids and a goat
all in that shack, or so people say.
Always, summer and winter,
three snow machines and at least
that many kids are scattered in the dooryard.
At school the kids all say the Hopper kids
have bugs and worms
(which they do)
and the kids don't get near them
except to call them names.

Well, listen, they're on welfare and food stamps
and every other give-away you can get.

I know it.
I wish to hell I could just sit around on my ass,
wouldn't have to work, just get handouts
and things like that.

Yeah, and I hear they got a couple of VCR's,
two stereos and everything.

And what about all those snow machines
they got around there all the time?

They get a new car about every six months, ya know.

Why, they got gold plated fixtures in the bathroom,
in the sink and shower both!

Somebody said they go down to Florida or some place
every winter and live in a big hotel
and on government money too!

People say
they're jealous, and
they say
them Hoppers have it good.

CAROL HOPPER

Almost any night you can see her on the street,
out to flee the noise and clutter of the shack,
her brothers, her mother's boyfriends.

Tonight, November 9, 8:00 P.M., thirty-eight degrees,
an inch of snow in the village, the highway wet,
headlights and streetlights glistening
in the road's black mirror.

There is a quiet here Carol comes to meet,
to be with, almost every night. She sits
in the dark on the steps of the abandoned
Farney place. She is sixteen, her long blond hair,
alight in streetlamps, is prettier than her face.

Trucks shift down and grind through the village,
westward and eastward, their red and yellow,
square-rigged lights vanish in the dark
and Carol Hopper listens to the engines fade.

SAM HINES AND THE CHRISTMAS MITTENS

About a week or so before Christmas last year
I saw Sam Hines down to Jerry's Garage one morning
and while we were visiting he said: Look at these!
And he held his hands out palms up to show me
a new pair of deerskin choppers with hand-knit liners
made of brown wool.

The kids give 'em to me for Christmas.
Little Sam bought the choppers with the money he
made sugarin' last spring and Jenny knit the liners.
I got 'em now because they couldn't wait. Ain't those
the nicest pair you ever seen?

A few days after that Sam and all the other parents
in town came down to the school for the Christmas
open house and exercises. When Sam went to leave,
his mittens were gone.

Then a couple weeks later Sam was driving through
the village and saw the littlest Hopper boy walking
down the road with a pair of mittens on so big
one of them could have been his hat.

Sam pulled over, rolled his window down and said:
Nice lookin' mittens.

You mean these? Yeah, nice ones, ain't they?

Where'd ja get 'em?

My mother give 'em to me fer Christmas!
She even knit the liners, see?

Yes, sir, those are *fine* mittens.
Nicest pair I ever seen.

And he rolled up his window and drove away.

THE BUDDHAS OF JUDEVINE

Life is suffering.
Siddhartha Gautama

I

When it was clear he couldn't keep on going,
Sam Hines quit the farming he had known his entire life—
and his father had known before him—and Sam Hines
turned his hand to carpentry and spent his life
until the age of fifty at that trade.

His life as carpenter came abruptly to an end the day
he fell from a scaffolding and hurt his back in a way
which meant he'd never climb a ladder again. After that
he spent his days, and tried to make a living, working wood
inside his shop inside the barn which stands beside the house
where years before he—and years before that his father—
had milked cows.

His life as woodworker also came abruptly to an end
the day the table saw took not only
the piece of wood he was working with,
but took also all the fingers and the thumb of his right hand.
By the time he felt the pain all his fingers and his thumb
were dangling like the relaxed talons of a hawk,
his fingers and his thumb held on only by strips of skin.

He cradled his right hand in his left, got into his truck,
put his right hand and its detached fingers in his lap and
drove himself the fifteen miles to the hospital whereupon
having gotten himself checked in, he fainted.

Five days later, after being transferred to Burlington,
after having two ten-hour operations to reconnect
bone, sinew, tendon, cartilage, nerve, muscle and skin,
he left the hospital and upon his leaving, said
to the surgeons who had put him back together again:

Well, boys, I just got to go. I know you need me awfully,
which is why I want you all to know,
I hate to have to leave you so shorthanded.

II

Because the surgeons were able to save only portions
of each finger, now each finger is a different length
and the entire hand so stiff, especially in cold weather,
that it's really not prehensile anymore. It can't close around
a hammer or a saw and it is hard, at the age of sixty,
to learn to be left-handed.

Yet Sam goes on: inventing a gadget for planting seedling trees,
repairing chairs, sugaring and, most importantly:
I got enough left of this one here
to hook it around and pull the trigger
so I can still hunt deer.

III

Sam's wife, whose name is Beatrice and who is another vessel
of kindness and long suffering sailing this sea of adversity,
has diabetes and has had a leg removed just below her knee.
She's confined to a wheelchair.

She wears gloves, even in the house and even in the summer,
because her hands are always cold. She wheels around the house
and kitchen, helps Sam get the meals,
does whatever else she can.

When I visit them in the kitchen, Beatrice in her wheelchair,
Sam in a straight chair, his hands and forearms resting on the table,
the two of them seated beside each other,
it seems to me they are the giant Buddhas of Polonaruwa:
their sad eyes simple, clear, straightforward,
their smiles filled with every possibility, questioning nothing,
rejecting nothing, accepting everything, their lives saying:
everything is emptiness, everything is compassion.

I can hear *The Bhagavad Gita* say:

> *Whatever you do, make it an offering to Me*
> *The food you eat, the worship you perform,*
> *The help you give, even your suffering.*

It is awe-ful and wonder-ful to me
how they carry their lives so nobly,
with such beauty and grace, as if
their suffering had become
garlands of sweet flowers
laid across their shoulders.

IV

I saw Sam just last week coming home across the field toward his
   house, back from Pond Brook where he had taken his limit.

After we had visited awhile and I'd asked about fishing
and then about his hand, he got to telling stories of the surgeons
who worked on him and he concluded saying:

Well, they did the best they could, and half a hand
is better than none. You'da liked them boys, David,
they was awful nice: just as ordinary as you are.

✦ ✦ ✦

COROT'S POOL

to the memory of my friend Millen Brand

Dawn. A summer morning,
and I am fishing on the river in Corot's Pool
which is just upstream from Singing Bridge,
a bridge with iron grating on which your tires sing.
I call this place Corot's Pool because
it is a broad, still, deep stretch of water with overhanging trees
and the hand-laid stone abutments of an old bridge on either side,
and on a sunny summer morning the light through the trees falls
upon the water and makes a dappled quietude of irresistible
    tranquility.
It is the kind of place where Corot would be if he were here
    instead of me.

Just a half-mile below, two hundred years ago,
Seth Hubbell watched
as the Providential Kindness of his Benefactor lifted his oxen
from this same river. Now I, without oxen, knowing a poverty
which is wealth compared to those who came before and with
a languid attitude toward work which makes the forebears twist
in their graves and my neighbors twist in their beds, and is one
of the reasons for my poverty, I cast a fly across the water, then
watch the sky more than the river. I can hear the cry of an osprey
out to find her breakfast. But I neither hunt nor work; instead

I climb out of the river and sit down in the morning light
on the quarried stone of an abutment, pour a cup of coffee
from my thermos, and relax from what was already relaxation
and I think.

The farmers on the hills and in the bottomland
are already at their morning chores.
In the village everything is quiet, but soon

just across the meadow and over the railroad tracks from here,
Roy McInnes will move from house to shop,
swing open the doors of doors and begin the day.
Soon also, down in the middle of the village,
Jerry will descend the stairs, open the garage
and roll his washing machine-flowerpot out toward the gas pumps.
Edgar Whitcom and Laura Cate, in their separate houses,
will rise, prepare their separate breakfasts,
and go about the things they do
to get themselves ready for another day.

These are good thoughts to me,
and, in spite of all that could be wrong and is,
I feel comfortable, at home in this place, in Judevine,
and here—where I am just now,
beside the river, in the morning light,
where it is so easy to see our lives
flowing through this place as the river flows.
All of us, together, here and always leaving,
just passing through.

And then I dream.

In my dream I see a sudden flash as if the sun exploded.
Then a wave in the air so great it crushes everything,
buildings, trees—all pushed instantly down.
And heat. Singing Bridge melts and drops
into the river. It sizzles in the water, a crumpled, twisted
corpse of steel. Then dark. The air filled with dust, debris
so dark it blots the sun. The mountains, all of them
on fire, the whole world on fire. Now a wind,
worse than any hurricane, blows down the valley.
Then nothing but a silence and everything destroyed.

A black rain falls, streaks the sooty ruins, puts out the fires.

I see my wife, her lithe and sensuous body,
the body I knew again and again, lying face down,
one arm stretched out, her beauty melted into the ground.

I see my son, fourteen years old, wandering dazed and burned,
down a cratered road strewn with fallen trees. I call to him.
He looks at me and doesn't answer.
His flesh drips from his fingers.

I see my daughter, three years old, who once skipped and sang
across the living room of my house, lying on her side,
her naked flesh purple as a newborn, as a beet.
She is convulsed by keloid shivers.
I bend down to touch her face and her face comes off
as if it were a mask, yet she remains
unmoving, shivering there—on her side.
Then she vomits once and long
and her body doesn't shiver anymore.

I see the river choked with bodies, bodies of trout,
bodies of beaver, otter, deer, muskrat, birds, the osprey,
people—people I knew, talked with, lived with, played with
here in Judevine—now so disfigured
I don't even know who they are.

There was a man calling to me from the river,
his hand outstretched to me. I reached for it, took hold,
the flesh slipped away as if it were a glove
and he disappeared into the water.

There are people wandering through the village,
the sockets of their eyes hollow, dark; their melted eyes
slather down their faces. They wander, arms stretched out,
in silence, everywhere, in silence, the silence broken only
now and then by the quiet cry: Water. Water.

Silence. No moaning, no weeping, no screaming in pain—
just silence and occasionally the quiet cry: Water. Water.

I see a man and a woman, both naked,
the pattern of their clothing stenciled on their bodies,
their bodies burned, their open sores oozing.
They are carefully and slowly propping up the branches
of the only remaining tree; they are carefully and slowly
wrapping rags around its barkless trunk.
It's Laura Cate and Edgar Whitcom.

And there are others wandering and vomiting,
holding their aching heads,
diarrhea squirting from their anuses,
their bodies consumed by chills and fever.

Everywhere: the dead, contorted shapes.
Judevine is dead.
All the birds and beasts of forest and stream,
all the people: dead.

We, love, were not water, not
always here and always leaving.

We were gone.

The dream is done. I wake. Judevine still here,
Corot's Pool here, the river here.
Less than a mile away the village wakes;
all is as it was, yet
all is changed.

We step into the day, all of us,
with this dream that hovers over us

and waits.

✦

Ah, bah gosh, David, I didn't t'ink I see you here.
Dis be da kinda mornin' be in a place like dis.
Oh! you got coffee. Here I'll drink a little of it for you.

Wall, David, since we be da two of us togedder here
we may as well go fishin'.
Dis place ain't no good no more, it used to be,
but it ain't no more. I know annuder hole just up da stream
is where we catch 'em good. You get your rod aroun' dat hole,
an', Mister, he gonna stiffin up an' come alive
an' jomp aroun' like you never see!
Let's go up dere where da fishin's good
an' see how we can do.

Like dat time, do you remember? when we poach
does trout outta Doc's pond up above da Lutter lot,
all dose years ago, do you remember?

PART III

GHOSTS

Dangling from a branch
nine feet off the ground
in a balm of Gilead
that stands beside the mill
below the road
down by the river
in the center of the village
is a baby carriage
which is the high-water mark
for the flood of '70
and is why nobody has ever
taken it down—a reminder
of the day we were cut off.
We paddled a canoe down the road to Jerry's
tied up at the gas pumps
and watched cars and porches
going down the river.
Nelson Beaudry got twelve trout
out of his cellar that day,
but that high water was nothing
like the flood of '27.
Then the river washed this place away
and some people say
what was left and what's here now
isn't a town at all.
They say it's only ghosts of what once was.
The only people who think this place is real,
they say, are folks who live here;
the rest of the world doesn't even see it,
drives through and doesn't notice—which
they say
is proof
Judevine and all of us who live here
really don't at all,

that we and this place are dead
and have been dead
for years.

TOMMY

Tommy Stames spent eighteen months in Vietnam. Pleiku, Hue.
Names strange, not at all like Judevine.
He was a hero when he got home.
Folks around here were proud of him, or if they weren't
they didn't say so. He had done his duty
and that was that.
Don't doubt it. It is true.
Everybody tried to make him feel at home
in his home. Some said he was nervous;
he had changed. Or maybe it was they
who moved around him circling at a distance
like dogs around a bear, wondering
what it was was in their midst.

When deer season came, Tommy got his deer,
as he had always done, every year, since he was twelve.
He had been the greatest hunter on the hill
and now everybody knew he was somehow even greater.
One shot dropped his buck, as always, and,
as always, as the seven times before,
he dressed his deer in the accustomed way,
opening the belly from sternum to vent,
his knife slipping cleanly through the hide and flesh.
Then a new maneuver.

His knife rung the genitals, extracting penis
and the testicles and with them a tab of belly skin.
He hung them by the fleshy ribbon in a tree

just as he had done
in Vietnam.

When the people heard of it, the men snickered and said
they'd have to try that next year
and the circle widened and we moved at a distance,
like dogs around a bear, wondering
what it was was in our midst.

GRACE

Grace lives in a trailer on the edge of town,
down along the river. She's got three kids.
She had a husband, but he split.
I saw a questionnaire once that she'd filled out
asking if they'd volunteer at school.
Here is what she said:

I'd like to but I got no time.
We get up at half past five, my husband and myself I mean
and he is out the door by 6:15.
Then I get up the kids and them and me all leave
together a little after seven.
I take Doreen to school, then drop the other two
to Mrs. Fairchild's and then I go to work myself.
When I get done I pick up the kids to Fairchild's
and we get home by six.
My husband, he gets home about an hour later.
By the time we get our supper there's no time left for nothin'.
We live like this six days a week, even Saturdays,
and Sundays we try to work around the place,
you know,
get in the wood or fix the goddamned car.

Since her husband left she's given up her full-time job
and things for Grace and for the kids have gone downhill,
which is no doubt one of the reasons she got into so much trouble,
but . . . Grace will speak for herself.

The hell I will.

Well, she *can* speak for herself.

You're goddamned right I can.

Will you? Please.

I got nothin' to say.

You do too.

Why do you want me to do this anyway?

It's your chance to have your say, to tell your side
and tell it like you want it told.

Why should I bother?
Nobody listens anyway.

I will.

Big fuckin' deal.

Thanks.
Are you going to tell your story?

Alright.
Alright, Mr. Poet, only
maybe you won't like it.

Maybe.

It ain't no Vermont picture postcard.

Good.

I suppose you want to hear about the time I had to go to court.

That'd be a good place to start.

Voyeur, ain't ya?

Yes. Just like everybody else.

True enough. Only everybody else don't write it down.
Where the hell do you get off, anyway, undressing all of us
    in public?
I've heard about those poems you write.
I've heard that's what you do.
I know how you do it. Fiction. Fiction, shit. I can barely read,
but I know fiction. Those people read your stuff really think
you made us up?

I made up you.

Bullshit to that! How could you?
I'm talkin' to you, ain't I?
Christ, you're stupider than I thought!

Are you going tell your story or stand around and dump on me?

Maybe I'll do both.

Fine!

You just want me to embarrass myself don't you?

No! I just want you to have your chance!

Alright. Alright. But nobody will listen.
Nobody around here ever listens. Everybody around here. . . .

You already said that.

Shut up! I'm talkin' ain't I?
Everybody around here already knows what they think of me.
They think I'm a beast or somethin'. They think
I'm not sorry for that time. Well, maybe I'm not. Huh?
Maybe I'm not sorry. How about that?
I didn't mean to hurt her. She's my baby, ain't she?
For Christ's sake, she came out of me.
All I wanted was some quiet. What's so wrong with that?
She was screaming, I mean screaming.
She'd been doing it for days.
You can only stand so much of that you know.
I stood as much as I could stand and then I hit her.
I hit her and I hit her and I hit her. I wanted to. . . .
Do you understand?
No. No. You don't. Because you can't, because
you are always in control, you always got yourself together.
No. You couldn't understand. You could never understand.
I love my baby. I love her and
I wanted to break her face.
Both. Both. Both those things!
Not just one. Goddamnit, not just one.
That's what I told the judge, but he's just like you.

Anymore on that?

No.

What . . . what about the way they say you sleep around?

164

Gimme a break will you, David?
Who says that? Edith? Christ.
How could I? When? You know what my life is like.
I would if I could, if I ever got the chance.
Why not? You think I'm made of stone or somethin'?
You think I wouldn't like to have somebody I could be with,
share all my troubles with, do chores and keep this place
together with? You think I wouldn't like that?
To have somebody to sleep up next to, to hold on to?
You're goddamned right, Mister, because it's comfort.
It's warm and good, I mean, sometimes it can be.

Fun. Fun is what I mean. Some fun!
We could stay at home all day some day
in the middle of the week,
just him and me, and lounge around all morning,
have lunch together,
take a bath and get in bed and make love and stay in bed
together, naked, and watch TV all afternoon
until the kids come home from school.

You don't think I'd like that? By Jesus, you *are* a fool.
You and everybody else in this goddamned place.
I hate this place! I hate it. And I hate you.
I'd get out of here tomorrow if I could.
I'd go some place if there was some place I could go.
I'd take the kids and go. I mean it.
I don't care what people say. To hell with them,
and you, and this goddamned place too.
Vermont! Vermont. Fuck Vermont.
And fuck you too. I'm not sayin' any more.

BOBBIE

For years Bobbie drove the pickup truck to Morrisville
every day to sew the flies in men's pajamas at a factory
down there. When you spoke to her about the job,
she'd blush and turn on her heel like a little girl.
She was good. The best one down there.
It was piecework and she was fast.
She quit the sewing when she and Doug went to farming.

Bobbie is beautiful, or could be.
Under thirty years of work and plainness you can see
her body, see her face,
those definite, delicate features
glowing.
She strides like a doe.
In spite of two brown teeth
her smile is warm and liquid.

Last summer she cut off a finger in the baler,
paid her farmer's dues.

Now she holds her missing finger behind her when she talks.
She's got something new to blush for.

DOUG

Last summer Doug pastured horses down at Sally Tatro's
in the village. He had eight down there.
One of the two big workhorses, the mare of the team,
got an apple stuck in her throat. When Doug found her
she was lying in a swamp almost dead from suffocation.
Doug skidded her out of the wet place with his pickup.
Then he called the vet:

Doc Jeffers come up, said the only thing to do was shoot her.
I asked him if he'd do it. He said no.
I asked Roy and Jerry. Nobody would.
So I come got my gun and did it myself.
After I done it, I sat down and bawled like a baby.
We logged together two winters.

What Doug didn't tell me but what I found out later
was that after he killed the mare he stayed with her
all that afternoon and into the dark of that night.
He stayed with her until her eyes clouded, until
she got cold.

Doug's better than six feet,
weighs more than two hundred and fifty pounds.
He has a couple of teeth missing up front and his voice
is high and pinched. It doesn't belong to his body.
When Doug laughs he sticks his enormous stomach out,
throws his head and shoulders back and laughs loud,
with his mouth open, like a picture I saw once
of a Russian peasant in *The Family of Man*.

Until recently Doug jumped from job to job
never keeping one more than a couple of months.
But he always had work. People hated him for that,
and for his saying:

I try not to work too much in the winter.
Gets in the way of my snow machinin'!

Like Edith says: Shiftless bum's what he is. On'y thing
he ever done regalar
is eat.

Doug has cut logs and pulp,
worked at the Firestone store in Barre,

167

been a mechanic in Burlington,
worked for the highway and the railroad,
been a farmer, a carpenter, hauled used brick,
sold barn boards and beams, trucked gravel, pumped gas,
driven a school bus, cut brush at Christmastime
and worked on the lifts for the Mountain Company,
and in all the years I've known him,
he's never been fired. He always quits.

No sir, I ain't doin' it!

Fine. Fine. If that's the way you want it,
that's the way you got it too!
I spent the winter eatin' snowballs lots of times before, ya know.

Fine! That's fine with me, 'cause I already quit! I quit!
But let me tell you one more thing before I'm out of here.
Mister Man, you shit in your hat and pull it over your ears!

Doug worked on the lifts when Jerry, Conrad and Arnie did.
They drove to work together; eighty miles a day round trip
so they could stand on top the state
and freeze their asses for two and a quarter an hour;
all day on top the mountain bowing and smiling,
helping New York ladies off the lifts.

Doug told me once how they got the turkeys:

Well, hell, we had to do somethin' to entertain ourselves!
As the chair topped the rise, we'd reach out, offer the skier a hand.
That was our job!
Then, at just the right moment, we'd give a little jerk
and down the turkey would go.

Oh! Pardon me ma'am! Excuse me! You alright?

Then we'd help her up, grab a little tit,
get her goin', step on the back of a ski, and down she'd go again!

Jerry Willey worked up there with us too, that little dink.
All he ever talked about was gettin' in their pants.
Well, I seen plenty of 'em up there I wouldn't mind tryin' out too.
But I never did, and Jerry, he never did neither.
That's a differ'nt class naow, ain't it?

After Granny died Doug and Bobbie started farming her old
    place. But the milk check is too small.
They can't get by on only cows.
Unemployment's up to 15 percent and Doug doesn't find jobs
the way he used to.

The last time I saw him he looked serious and sad.
He asked me, *me*, if I knew of any work.
I haven't seen him throw his stomach out,
his head and shoulders back, and laugh
in a long time.

ENVOY TO DOUG

Doug told me once
he always wanted to go to college,
study, get a certificate,
be a math teacher
in a school somewhere.
He likes kids. Everybody knows that.

We've got a new roller rink down in Morrisville now
and it turns out Doug's the best one there.
Six foot, two hundred fifty pounds, the biggest pot
you've ever seen, but he moves across the floor

so light it seems he isn't even touching.
He can skate backwards, do a spin.

When he and Bobbie start to dance
everybody watches. They glide and twirl.
Bobbie smiles her shy smile
then Doug draws away on one skate,
a loop, a spin, alone across the floor.
You can hear his squeaky laugh rise
above the noise of skate wheels and organ.

He spreads his arms and legs apart
and floats across the floor smooth
as cream   his body   open   leaning
on the air.

GOSSIP AT THE RINK

The organ stops and the skaters glide off the floor,
and those there from Judevine are drawn toward each other
by some kind of communal bond in the presence of so many
    strangers,
all that is, except Grace and Tommy who have also come here
this afternoon, but now keep a distance from the others.

As Bobbie and Doug undo their skates
Conrad wobbles up to them.

Way ta go, Dougie, way ta go. I want to tell ya, you skate good.

You ain't so bad yourself, Conrad.

Well, thing is, I can skate, but I can't twirl like you can.
You're good at twirlin', Doug.

You should practice.

Well, I dunno about that.
Ho! Speakin' a twirls, here comes Edith.
Hi, Edith, how you doin'?

No better.

Figures.

I guess you could see how Grace was hangin'
all over that Tommy Stames here this afternoon.

I'm kinda glad . . .

Slobberin' all over each other, right now,
out there in the parkin' lot.

I'm kinda glad to see them two together.

I think it's disgusting.

God, you think everything's disgusting, Edith.

You can make all the fun you want, Doug . . .

Why, thank you, Edith, I think I will!

but I heard they're shackin' up together.

I know they are, Edith.

They been livin' together about a month now, Edith.
By the Jesus, Conrad, Edith here is slippin'.
She ain't keepin' her ear tight enough to the ground!

I know it! Hey, Edith,
you got to keep that thing pressed tight
if you're gonna keep up with the news!

Go ahead you two, but you'd think she'd have
a little shame or modesty or something
after that awful trial.

It was a hearin', Edith, not a trial; it was a hearin'
and it was a long time ago.

Well, I think the two of them hitchin' up together
is gonna be nothin' but T-R-O-U-B-L-E.

Why is that, Edith?

You know very well why, Conrad.
Vietnam did something to that boy's inside brain.
You heard what he did with that deer up in the woods.

What'd he do, Edith? What'd he do?
I want to hear you spell it!
What'd he do?

It's no use with the two of you.
There are children involved here.
I'm thinking about the children.

Gawd!

You're thinking about yourself, Edith, like you always do.

That boy is a potential madman.

Why he's not!

He's a sick boy! He's a stick of dynamite
ready to go off in somebody's face!

He's a good man!

Calm yourself, Edith, calm yourself! You're off the handle!
I see Tommy with them kids and he treats 'em good.
He loves them kids just like he does Grace. You can tell.

There are lives at stake here, children's lives!
Why, you know what they do. They lie around all day
up in that trailer naked and drink beer and smoke dope!

Yeow! It sounds like heaven to me!

You know they're doin' that.

Conrad, they're doin' that!

They're doin' what?

They're doin' that!

They're doin' that ?

Oh, my God, they're doin' that!

I wish ta hell I was doin' that!
Beats roller skatin', don't it, Bobbie?

I am thinking of this community.
I am just standing up for what is right!

Oh, sure, sure you are.
And you're an authority on what's right, too, aren't ya, Edith?
Why, of course you are. Why . . .

you watch that Bill Donahue show!

It is not Bill. It is Phil.
What's the matter? You got trouble with *your* inside brain?

Hey! I ain't got cable.

That's not all you ain't got.

Edith, why don't you leave them two alone?
Probably they got troubles of their own.
Why don't you do somethin' else with all your extra spare time.

Yeah, like, why don't ya learn ta skate.
Learn ta skate, Edith. Save us all and learn ta skate.

Bobbie, I'm surprised at you. Why don't you speak up?
This is a terrible thing that is happening here.

Come on, Bobbie, let's go home.

I agree with you, Edith.

What?

I agree with her!

You would.

All you guys ever think about is Grace.
I'm thinking about the kids!

That's right.

Jesus. Two of a kind.

And I don't like all that dirty talk either.

Gawd! for awhile there I thought we were havin' fun.
You sure know how to ruin a good time!

Snip, snip, snip, all the time, Edith. Fer God's sake!
Snip, snip, snip. Come on, Bobbie.
Snip, snip, snip. Jesus Christ, Edith. Snip, snip, snip.

Bobbie, Doug and Conrad abandon Edith, leaving her alone.

Out in the parking lot, in Tommy's car, Tommy and Grace
are drinking beer and Southern Comfort, when Tommy says:

I . . . ah . . . I made a little poem for you.

You did?

Yeah . . . you wanna hear it?

Sure.

It's called "A Fleeting Animal."

A FLEETING ANIMAL

When you abandon everything
   and give yourself to me
when I abandon everything
   and give myself to you
we make a fleeting animal

of such beauty, passion,
   nakedness and grace
that I am glad it slips away
   when we are done
because this world is hurt
   and cruel and nothing
that naive and loving
   and unashamed
could possibly survive.

✦ ✦ ✦

PULP CUTTERS' NATIVITY
A DREAM IN TWO ACTS

ACT ONE

Christmas Eve morning: just after dawn.
The sun is not yet up.
The temperature is twenty degrees below zero.

Here, at the upper end of Bear Swamp, in a far corner
of Judevine, not far from Raymond and Ann's:
the landing of a pulpwood operation.
Piles of softwood pulp: balsam, spruce, some hemlock
and a little pine.

Close to the road: the logs full-length, waiting to be bucked.
A peavey leaning on a log. Nearby
an old, dilapidated crawler tractor.
Fifty-five gallon drums of gas and oil and smaller cans
of gas and oil for chain saws. There:
two pulp hooks, stuck into the ends of logs,
and over there a pile of empty beer cans, plastic bags
and other litter. Right here: the blackened remains
of yesterday's fire. And snow everywhere.
At the landing here the snow is mixed
with wood chips, bark and dirty oil.

Now far off, a couple miles away,
a car coming up the road
clearly heard in this cold and crystalline
winter-morning air.

Then the car pulls in, shuts down. ANTOINE *gets out*
and immediately begins to build a fire from the litter
of scraps and butt ends that are everywhere.

He sprinkles a little gasoline, then some dirty oil
over the pyramid of wood, strikes a match, jumps back
and watches the fire begin to roar.
He holds his hands out to the fire, then turns around
bends over, pulls up his coat and warms his ass.
He paces in front of the fire hugging and slapping himself,
banging his mittened hands together,
hopping back and forth from foot to foot,
exhaling like a workhorse.

ANTOINE: Shitacat'sass! Freeze like a turd!
        Bull an' jam here outin da snow,
        so cold touchhole fall right out!

        An' dese pants ain't wut' two cents,
        so ain't dis discount jacket
        an' dese boots got cracks
        from las' year. May as well be out here
        dressed in my bikini.
        Freeze like a turd.

        I'm gettin' old. I can't take dis
        too much longer. And den what I do?
        Live on dat friggin' Social 'curity?
        'baout enauf buy a can a peacesoup once a mont'.

        I work longer dan the sun . . . you lazy basterd!

        I be here 'fore you get oudda bed,
        be here still when you gone home!

        An' fer what? Make friggin' fifty, eighty dollar
        a week, tear my gut out for dat?
        An' I work forenoon Saturday
        just for da gover'munt. Da snooty basterds
        take it all! Every friggin' penny.

        I be better off collect da check,

stay to home, sit by da stof
rock away da winner
like I use' ta be.

It ain't no use. I never get ahead.
Da friggin' politicians tax da pants
right off my wimens. I got naut'in'!
I never had naut'in'. My Poppa,
he never had naut'in'.
Why, by da Jesus, I'm so poor
I can't afford to cast a shadow.

I tell dat to dem Washin'tonians dey say:
Dat's okay. We take it!
An' fer what? So dey can waltz araound
down dere an' fuck dere sec'ertarie
'steada eatin' lunch? Fuck me!
It be a goddamn miracle sent down by God
da likes a me ever make a decent livin'.

T'ieves, all of 'em. Bad acters, ever' one.
No-counts. Two-cylinders.
Robbers what dey be, 'ceptin you can't tell it
'cause dey wear a suit!

Now you take some poor basterd
up in dis godforsaken place, let 'im steal
a chain saw or a caow, see what happen!
Lock 'im up right naow!
Mister Man, I mean right naow!
An' why dey do dat?
Cause he be a t'ief? Poof!
Dey lock 'im up 'cause he be stupid!
He be too daum ta wear a suit!

Okay. You take me. Say I write my senater,
say: I'm sorry, sir, but I be too poor
ta pay da taxes so don't you bodder

send da bill. I wake up nex' mornin'
in da clinker wid da chicken t'ief,
an' my wimens and da babies be alone.

An' ones we got right here to home,
da ones daown to state capitol,
is even worse. Caum time dey be elected
dey caum 'raound shake my hand say:
I work for you, I be your sla'f
daown to da capitol. Talk about straight
as serpent did to Eve. Den dey get elected
an' you see how dere noses get funny color
from bein' up da touchhole a da millionaires
too long. You see 'em on da street say:
Ho! I be Antoine, 'member me?
Dey push you 'raound like you be stick of pulp!

Ah, what's dah use? It never be no different
'an it be right now. It never wass. It never be.
No use. Piss and moan is all I ever do,
'cause it's all dere is for da likes of me.
At least it make me feel a little better some.
Preach at dis pile a wood.
fifty, eighty dollar a week,
an' a hernia every day! Shit.
Basterds. Crooks. Two-cylinders.
No use.

Bull an' jam. Freeze like a turd.

[*A car pulls up.* DOUG *gets out, slams the door,
and moves toward the fire.*]

By Jesus, where you been? It's
da middle of da afternoon.

DOUG: Couldn't drag myself outta bed.

180

My back is killin' me. That goddamn crawler
is about to do me in. Pinched a nerve or somethin'.
Hurts like hell.
And this weather don't help neither.

I always thought that Conrad was a crazy stupid fool,
but maybe he ain't; maybe he knows what he's talkin'
     'bout.
He was sayin' t'other day he thinks this ugly weather's
     'cause
of all that walkin' on the moon or 'cause
that air pollution's eatin' holes into the sky. Hell,
you know it's somethin' what ain't natural.

Two years ago it was so dry I got no hay a'tall.
Come this summer, I got hay standin' to my waist
but it's so wet ya couldn't drive a tractor down the road.
Ain't natural.

Spring comes too late, fall comes too early,
but it's worse than it ever used to be,
and the birds ain't actin' right.

Why, this September and October was wet as May and
     June, and now,
Christmas Eve and twenty below;
this is February weather! Ain't natural.

Too goddamn cold too soon!
Why, this morning when I stepped outside to blink
my eyeball froze right open
and my feet froze to my shoes!

ANTOINE: Ah, Dougie.

DOUG: It don't make it easy.

181

ANTOINE: Dat be da Bible troot'!

DOUG: Well, there's only one thing worse than all this crazy
      weather
and that's what's called the holy state of matrimony.
Holy, hell! It's like livin' with the devil!

You go out and get yourself a hen; she clucks around
for about a year or two, then she gets broody
and she begins ta cackle; you get too close that hen'll
peck ya. She'll sit around all day, watch them soaps
and all the time be eatin' up your money.

Christ, if I'da known I'da never done it.
It's a terrible price to pay for rollin' 'round the bed.
Jesus! how I wish I'd been smart like Tommy. Stay away
from church and all that marryin' stuff. I wish I'd been
like him. Stop in at night, see his little lady, dip in
and go. That kid is free!
He ain't locked inside a henhouse every night.

Hell, it's too late for me. I'm a domesticated cock,
and what's worse there's only one hen in my flock.

Sometimes I think that Albert's got the right idea.
Have five of 'em so you can be a decent rooster. But
every time I think that way I remember what he's got.
I'm locked up with only one, that poor bastard,
he's had five! No wonder he can't talk. Probably
they cut his tongue out, cut out t'other one too.
Some cock he is, can't crow or fuck;
no wonder he's so ugly.

By Jesus, I'm a slave for life,
but I can see it could be worse.

Listen boys out there, stay the fuck away from church.

Don't be like me and spend your life
wishin' you were someplace else and cryin'
to yourself 'bout how you didn't know how it would be.
Take it from me, she can catch you in a minute,
then she'll be done, but you'll have that chain
around your chicken leg for all your days!

You catch one and you think you've got
a sweet young thing, soft as a puffball on a tree.
You get her home and Mister you have got a witch!
She'll change into a bully spruce so rough
it hurts to look. And ugly! Christ!
you just don't know! She'll drink your booze
and eat your food, get fatter than a sow.
She'll piss and moan and scream at you.
She'll belch and fart and lock you out!

Don't do it boys! Don't you get caught!
By Jesus Christ, I wish to hell
I'd run until I'd lost her.

ANTOINE: Shitagoddamn! Soun' like you climb onto
        Canadian t'istle. A burr in your ass dis mornin'.
        I always taut your little wimens
        be gentle as a doe. What happen to you?

DOUG: Ah, things ain't workin' out just right.

ANTOINE: Wall, I be here to listen
        if you want to talk.

DOUG: It's nathin'.
        It'll all blow over, maybe.

        Where the hell is Tommy!
        Damn near seven o'clock.

If he'd work that dink a little less
and run the chain saw more
maybe we'd get somethin' done.

ANTOINE: Caum on now, Doug.
You take it easy on dat boy.
He be good worker and you know he be.
You wass a kid once too.

Caum on,
we warm our han's before we go to work.

[*Another car pulls up.* TOMMY *gets out and hurries to the fire.*]

TOMMY: Sorry I'm late. Hard to get up.
Christ, it's cold!
That bed is better than this place.

DOUG: Oh, sure it is, 'cause Grace kept sayin':
Don't go! Don't go! I want some more!
You sharpen them saws?

TOMMY: I sharpened 'em.

DOUG: Where's yours?

TOMMY: Down to the woods.
It didn't need it.
Only needed touchin' up.

DOUG: That's no surprise.
It don't dull if it don't cut!

TOMMY: Lemme alone, Doug.

ANTOINE: Tommy, he have bad night.
    His back is sore.

DOUG: That ain't it! We're losin' money
   with this equipment standin' here.
   We got to get goin'!
   And this kid here better make up his mind
   if he's gonna cut pulp or fuck around.
   He's been late all week!
   I ain't out here for my health you know.

TOMMY: I told you I was sorry about bein' late.

DOUG: Yer always sorry and yer always late!

ANTOINE: You boys stop dat naow!

    Dere be plenty time to cut da tree.
    Dey be here hunnert years,
    mus' be dey be here at least till noon.
    Dey ain't gonna raun away.
    You bot' sit daown, warm up by dis fire,
    den we all go to work.

DOUG: Where's that log truck? Where's Desjardins?
   We're plugged right up in here.
   I got no room to move around.
   When's he comin'? You call 'im, Antoine?

ANTOINE: Yas! Yas!
    He say he be here end da week!

TOMMY: Either one of you got anything to eat?
    I ain't had my breakfast yet.

DOUG: You hain't ettin' yet? Well, ain't that a shame!
       You're supposed to eat before you come!
       Shit, boy, this ain't a picnic!
       Why didn't you have your woman for breakfast?

ANTOINE: Doug.

DOUG: You're the one who's always sayin'
      how full of vitamins and minerals that stuff is.
      Ought to be you could go all day on just . . .

ANTOINE: DOUG!

TOMMY: You're leanin' on me hard, man.
       You'd better lighten up.

DOUG: Yeah?

TOMMY: Yeah. Really.

DOUG: Is that right?

TOMMY: Yeah. That's right.

DOUG: I seen those darkies you got hangin' around your place.

TOMMY: What are you talkin' about?

DOUG: I'm talkin' about those junglebunnies you got visitin' you.

TOMMY: What about 'em?

DOUG: Them your . . .
      soul brothers
      from Vietnam?

186

ANTOINE: Caum on, you two. Stop it naow.

TOMMY: Yeah. They are.
    That's exactly what they are.

DOUG: Well, we don't like niggers around here,
    and we don't like nigger lovers.

TOMMY: Is that right?
    You and who else.

DOUG: Me and that's enough!

ANTOINE: Stop it, Doug!

DOUG: Shut up, frog!

    Why don't you and your nigger friends
    go somewhere else? Why don't you take that cute little
    piece of pussy of yours and all them nigger friends
    and get the fuck out of here!

TOMMY: Oh, Jesus! why can't you wake up!
    We're all in this together!
    We're all gettin' fucked over in the same way!
    Can't you see that?

DOUG: What?

TOMMY: How come you never finished school?
    How come you're not a math teacher somewhere
    like you wanted to be? How come?

DOUG: What are you talkin' about?

TOMMY: I'm talkin' about
       you got more in common with those
       "nigger" friends of mine
       than you do with all those white folks
       you're always workin' for.

       I mean, people like you and me and my friends.
       We're together! The Man is after your ass too.
       Why can't you see that?

DOUG: Are you sayin' I ain't white? You sayin' I'm not white?
      You are fuckin' crazy, man. Edith's right. You're crazy.
      I'm white, Mister. I am white!

TOMMY: Yes. That's right.

DOUG: No black man is my friend.

TOMMY: That's right. You're right.

DOUG: I ain't no nigger and I ain't no gook.
      I am white!

TOMMY: That's right. You *are* white.

DOUG: [*to* ANTOINE] He's crazy.

ANTOINE: It's you!

[DOUG *turns his back on* ANTOINE *and* TOMMY
and walks away from the fire.]

       Let it go, Tommy.
       Caum on. I got saum breakfast here for you.
       Here's saum coffee an' saum bread

188

da wimens make last night,
and saum apple jelly, and . . .
Ah! and lookit here! I got a leg a chicken too.

Caum on, Tommy, eat. Eat, Tommy. Eat.

How be your little wimens?

TOMMY: Good.

ANTOINE: Good. You babies ever t'ink baout maybe you get
married?

TOMMY: We're talkin' on it.
But, Antoine, it's a scary thing,
especially for . . . well . . . you know . . .
for Grace and me.

ANTOINE: Wall, yas, I know,
but if you don't try to start again . . .
why be alive?

TOMMY: Yeah, well, we been talkin' on it
and pretty serious, too.

ANTOINE: Good. Dat be da t'ing to do: get married.
Better'an livin' to yourself, Tommy.
You need saumbody to be wid,
talk to, share. It get to be
like bein' just one person.
It's no good to be alone.

TOMMY: Jesus, don't I know.

ANTOINE: We were meant to go two by two.

TOMMY: Thank you, Antoine.
　　　　Well, I better get to work.

[TOMMY *heads for the woods.* DOUG *who has been watching from a distance, approaches* TOMMY.]

DOUG: Tommy. What I said. . . . That weren't right.
　　　I'm . . . sorry. I'm sorry, Tommy.
　　　It's just . . . we're earnin' nothing out here
　　　but our deaths! Ah! never mind.

[TOMMY *and* DOUG *turn away from each other, and* TOMMY *moves off into the woods. A car pulls up.* ARNIE *gets out.*]

ANTOINE: Ho! Look who it be!

DOUG: Aw, Christ, hang on to your wallet!
　　　Lock everything up! Here comes Arnie.

ANTOINE: Wall, Arnie, how you be?
　　　　What you up to 'sides no good?
　　　　Workin' naow?

ARNIE: Naw. Can't find nathin'.

DOUG: I bet you ain't lookin' too hard neither.
　　　Can't afford to have a job, old Arnie can't,
　　　always gettin' in the way of his goin' to jail.
　　　Christ, this county's goin' broke just buyin' grease
　　　to lubercate the jailhouse door
　　　he's in and out of there so much.

ARNIE: I was wonderin' if you could take me on.
　　　Things is terrible narrow just right now.

DOUG: Oh, no! Oh, no! Antoine, I'm warnin' you.
He comes, I go. I ain't workin' with him anymore.
We'll go broke just puttin' back all the stuff he steals.
That bastard'll steal the shirt right off your back,
won't ja, Arnie? Why not tell 'im
where you got that jacket?

ARNIE: Mountain Company give it to me
when I got done.

DOUG: Give it to you, shit.
You stole it and you know it.

ARNIE: Wall . . . I had it caumin'.

DOUG: Sure you did. So did we all.
Only maybe you should say how come
you got one big enough for me.

ARNIE: Only one I could get a holt of.

DOUG: Bullshit to that! You're a liar too.
That's the one you stole from me.
I ought to tear that thing right off your back
right now only I couldn't stand to touch it.
It smells too bad.

[DOUG *walks away again.*]

ARNIE: Ugly ain't 'ee.

ANTOINE: He ain't functionatin' right today.
Got a splinter in his pecker.

I wish we had a place for you, but just now

191

we ain't. Da boy down to da woods,
Doug bouncin 'raound on dat crawler
an' I be here at da landin'.
Nat'in' you could do. I wish dat we could
help you out. I don't know how long we be here
anyway. Dat crawler just about to come apart to pieces.
When dat happen we be done.

How be your little wimens? I hear da two of you
be back togedder.

ARNIE: Yas, we're back together, but it ain't no better.
Just like it used to be. She's just as ugly
as she always was. Mister, she drinks whiskey
like you used to drink that beer.
I'd be better off livin' with a bobcat.

ANTOINE: Wall, dat too bad. A man shouldn't haf to wear
his hard hat in da house.

ARNIE: I know, Christ, if I had the money
the first thing I'd do is buy her a funeral.

She's good fer nathin'. Last summer
she was sick every mornin'. Get up
puke out her guts. Eats like a pig too.
I never seen her be so fat as she is right now.

Wall, I won't keep ya.
Lemme know if you can use another hand.

ANTOINE: I will.

[ARNIE *begins to leave.*]

Arnie, . . . I be sorry.

[ARNIE *gets in his car and drives away.*
TOMMY *reappears from the woods, running, out of breath.*]

TOMMY: Somebody stole my saw!

ANTOINE: What you say?

TOMMY: Somebody stole my saw!
When I got down to where it was
it was gone and there's a fresh pair of tracks
leadin' away toward the swamp.

DOUG: Arnie! It was that friggin' Arnie!
Where's that maul? I'm gonna find that walkin'
piece of kindlin' wood and split 'im down the middle.

ANTOINE: Hold on der! How you know dat it be him?

DOUG: Goddamn you, you softhearted frog. You . . .

ANTOINE: You take your pecker out your mout'
put in a turd!

We're goin' lookin' but we're gonna cipher first.

TOMMY: I give two hundred for that saw!
I'm still payin' on it.

ANTOINE: Take it easy. We get it back.

DOUG: That's right and all we got to do
is go right over to Arnie's place to do it.

ANTOINE: Naow how he steal dat saw?
        He be here all dat time, right here wid us,
        just a little bitago talkin' 'baout a job.

TOMMY: Maybe he's workin' with somebody else
        and he was up here coverin' for the other guy
        keepin' us here while the other guy took it.

DOUG: Nah, Arnie's too stupid to think a that.

ANTOINE: You don't be so sure. Arnie ain't no dummy.
        His head ain't got much shape to it,
        but it got some brain inside. I know;
        I work wid him for years in da Christmas tree.
        He ain't as stupid as he looks.

TOMMY: Stick up your foot.

DOUG: Huh?

TOMMY: Stick up your foot!
        You too, Antoine.
        And whose track is that?

ANTOINE: Mus' be Arnie.

TOMMY: And that's the track is in the woods.

DOUG: Proof enough for you, Frenchman?

ANTOINE: Yas. Proof enauf for me.

TOMMY: Let's go.

DOUG: Bring a pulp hook, Tommy.

By Jesus, Mister, when I take a holt
that peckerhead an' squeeze
his brain pop out his skull
like a blackhead out a pimple!

ACT TWO

Later that same morning at ARNIE'S *house: a shack
inside and out. In the littered dooryard: junk.
Pieces of cars, a snow machine, a doghouse, a dog,
some tractor tires, an old refrigerator and piles of rusting, rotting,
unidentified rubble. The sagging porch is littered too.
Two garbage cans stand near the door filled and overflowing
with empty beer and whiskey bottles, a broken couch,
a broken TV set, some broken chairs stacked on top each other,
a clothesline across the porch and the clothes hanging
frozen stiff. And tacked to a post, a fresh coyote skin.*

*Inside: one room, in a corner an old, brown, sheet-metal
pot burner, in another a new, color console, TV set,
a couch, some chairs, a chrome-and-Formica kitchen table,
a white, metal kitchen sink, some metal cupboards,
a four-burner gas stove, a double bed,
no curtains on the windows and no shades,
a peeling linoleum rug.
The place is hot and smells of kerosene.*

GIL, ARNIE'S *wife, sits at the kitchen table drinking beer
and watching game shows on TV.
Arnie steps up slowly onto the porch.
He's carrying a chain saw.
He stops, looks back, then rattles the locked door.*

ARNIE: Open the goddamn door!

GIL: Who is it?

ARNIE: Open the friggin' door! Hurry up!

GIL: How's a woman 'sposed ta get her chores done
when she's got ta be raunin' back and forth
to the door all the time? A man's work's
from sun to sun, or so the sayin' goes,
only I wouldn't know since the lazy bastard I live with
never worked a day in his life,
but a woman's work is never done.
Who is it?

ARNIE: Hurry up! It's me.

GIL: Who?

ARNIE: Me!

GIL: You?

ARNIE: Yas, me!

GIL: Oh, you. Go away. I gotta watch my shows.
Take a walk in the swamp.

ARNIE: That's where I been!
Open the door. I got somethin' ta show ya.

GIL: Oh no you don't! I ain't openin' my door an'
you ain't showin' me a thing!

I ain't never seen anything like it.
He just can't stay away from me.

Ten o'clock in the mornin' and that's all he can think about.

Never seen anything like it.
Well, he ain't gettin' any.
I got my shows ta watch
and this afternoon I got ta watch the stories.

ARNIE: Open up, you ugly bitch.
    Quit pickin' at those dirty toenails and chewin' on 'em
    in your mouth and open the goddamn door!

GIL: See how he talks to me? Ugliest man
    whatever walked. Got no appreciation.
    Who is it cleans and cooks and sews?
    Who washes his pants and mends his clothes?
    Who cuts up his deer
    and buys him his beer?
    Who bakes him his bread
    and gets in his bed?
    He was damn near dead
    before I came back
    and this is the thanks I get.

    Ugly! Why, I ought ta leave him now, again.
    I'd do it too if it weren't he needs me so.
    Got no appreciation.

ARNIE: If you don't open this door . . .

GIL: Hold on to that smelly ass of yours!
    I'm caumin'!

    [GIL *opens the door and sees the saw.*]

    Where did you get *that!*

ARNIE: I got it. An' I can get a hunnert for it too
    over to Waterville.

GIL: You stupid fool! You must like it there
     down to the jail. What's the matter
     they cook better'an me?
     Well, I ain't bailin' you out again.
     I told you so the last time.
     You end up there once more,
     yer on yer own.

ARNIE: They ain't gonna get me.
       They don't know.
       I fooled 'em good. Besides
       by the time they figure it all out
       I'll have it sold.

GIL: Well you had better.

[GIL *looks out the window.*]

     Who's this now?

ARNIE: Huh?
       Oh shit! It's them.

GIL: Fooled 'em good, you say.
     Now what you gonna do?
     By the looks of 'em
     this ain't no ordinary visit.

ARNIE: Lock the door!
       What we gonna do!

GIL: What ya mean, we?

ARNIE: You're in this too.
       They'll bloody *both* our heads.

198

Think a somethin' quick!

GIL: Go get that little blanket over there
and wrap the saw up in it.
I'll get into the bed and put the saw in with me.
We'll say I had a baby just this mornin'.
They won't believe it,
but they'll be afraid ta look.

ARNIE: Good.

GIL: You sit down there, sing a lullaby
and try your hand at actin' natural.

[ARNIE *does as he is told.* ANTOINE, DOUG, *and* TOMMY
approach the shack and hear ARNIE *singing a lullaby mercilessly
out of tune.*]

ANTOINE: Mus' be we're too late.
I t'ink Arnie kill hisself.
I can hear 'im dyin'.

DOUG: Cut the jokes. This here's for blood.
Open this door you son of a bitch!

[GIL *moans.* ARNIE *moves to the door, opens it, puts
his finger to his lips:*]

ARNIE: Shhhhhhhh . . . she ain't too good.
She's feelin' awful poorly.
She had a baby boy this mornin'
while I was out
and I be the father.
Weren't just fat after all.

DOUG: Better think a somethin' better'an 'at, you little dink.
You know why we're here.

ARNIE: I do?

ANTOINE: Seemzo Tommy here got his saw stolt—

ARNIE: Naw!

ANTOINE: —an' we t'ink da t'ief be you.

ARNIE: Come on, now, Antoine, you know me,
would I do a thing like that?

DOUG: You bet your ass you would!

ARNIE: You hurt my feelin's Doug, but have a look around.
You ain't gonna find nathin'. And keep your voices down
I'm wicked upset about how she is. I'd rather die
'an see her hurt that way.

[GIL moans.]

GIL: Who is it, dear? Who are those men?

ARNIE: Don't pay no mind ta her; she's outin her head in pain.
She just had it, just a little bit ago.
She ain't even cut the cord.

TOMMY: Sure she ain't, because a saw won't start without it.

[The pulp cutters search the house but stay clear of the bed.]

ARNIE: You boys want a beer?
How about some food.

200

Got a nice new doe down cellar,
fry you up a steak.

TOMMY: We don't want nuthin' but my saw!

ARNIE: What's the matter? Ain't our stuff good enough for ya?

GIL: Honey, can't you make them leave? I've got
ta get some sleep. I'm all wor' dout.

ARNIE: You boys ought to be ashamed!
Your hearts should break.
We don't need this now.
I swear that we be tellin' you the truth
and here's my deal I give as proof;
if we be lyin' I'll go out
and *sell* this child,
my firstborn son.

[GIL *moans*.]

Come on now, why don't ja go?

ANTOINE: I can't find a t'ing.

DOUG: Me neither.

TOMMY: I give two hundred for that saw.

DOUG: Com'on, Tommy, we may as well go back
an' start trackin' in the swamp.

[DOUG *and* TOMMY *leave*.]

ANTOINE: Wall, we be terrible sorry t'ink you be da one.

I apologize for allahus.

I hope you feelin' better, Gil. I know
you be; just get saum sleep. An' I be awful glad
to hear 'bout dat little baby. Congratulations
to you bot'.

DOUG: Com'on, Antoine!

[ANTOINE *leaves.* GIL *hops out of bed.*
GIL *and* ARNIE *are delighted with themselves.*]

DOUG: Goddamnit, I just know that saw is there!
That whole thing was just a lie.

ANTOINE: Wall, maybe so, but maybe not.
You boys give dat baby anyt'ing?

DOUG: You kiddin' me? The only thing I'd give 'im be
a knock onto his old man's head an' dump him out
behind the barn.

TOMMY: I give two hundred for that saw.

ANTOINE: You boys wait here. I wanna give dat baby somet'ing.

[ANTOINE *returns to the shack and knocks on the door.*]

ARNIE: Oh Christ! They're back.

[GIL *grabs the saw and hops back into bed.*
ARNIE *goes to the door, opens it and shouts:*]

Go away!

ANTOINE: Don't get me wrong. Da odders ain't be here.
I just caum back ta give da baby saumt'ing.
All I got's a quarter but at least it be saumt'ing.

I sure would like to see dat little skipper.

[ANTOINE *steps in.*]

ARNIE: No! . . . You can't.
Don't look! He's . . .
deformed!

ANTOINE: Well, dat's alright.

ARNIE: He didn't come out right!

ANTOINE: I don't mind.

ARNIE: He's all skund up!
Don't look. Oh please don't look!
It's awful. It'll make you sick.

ANTOINE: I jus' wan' a little look, eh?

[ANTOINE *moves quietly toward the bed
and gently pulls the covers back.*]

Ow! He got a long snout!

[ANTOINE *picks up the saw and cradles it in his arms
as if it were a baby.*]

Wall, maybe he be hugly but he be yours
an' now you got to love 'im.
Hey boys! Caum over, see da baby!

[DOUG *and* TOMMY *enter.*]

How you like da little t'ing?

DOUG: You bastard!
I'm gonna put this pulp hook up your ass!

TOMMY: Not if I do it first!

[DOUG *and* TOMMY *wrestle with each other for the pulp hook.*]

I want that pulp hook, you big, fat, racist pig!

DOUG: You do, do ya?
Well, you ain't gettin' it you white liberal, dope-smokin',
pussy-lickin', left-wing, commie, pinko, faggot!

TOMMY: Oh, yeah?

DOUG: Yeah!

ANTOINE: Oh, Mary, Mudder a' God, Saint Jude and Saint Teresa
not dis again!

[*There is an odd pause here in which, for reasons only*
TOMMY, DOUG, *and God know,*
both men step outside themselves, break into smiles and see
the absurdity and hilarity in their situation.]

TOMMY: Actually, that weren't bad Doug. Pretty good really.
Only like I said before: I want that pulp hook
you peckerheaded, ofay, honky, redneck,
fat jigglin', slab-sided
obese and obnoxious blob of white trash!

DOUG: Is zat so! You think you're man enough ta get it?
       You nigger-lovin', chink-food eatin',
       pacifistic, hippie disgrace
       to the sovereign state of Vermont!

TOMMY: Oh, yeah?

DOUG: Oh, yeah!

ANTOINE: Stop it! Stop it naow!
          Stop dat talk in front da baby!
          And quiet your voices down too.
          Can't you see da little skipper's sleepin'?

TOMMY: Yeah, he sure is quiet and peaceful, ain't he?
        Yet look how rugged he already is;
        tougher 'an a piece a steel.

DOUG: That's no surprise, probably Arnie's already got 'im
       doin' chores. Yeah, he's ruggid alright,
       and that's the only difference, otherwise
       he looks just like his father!

ANTOINE: Yas, he do, and I never see a baby be so young
          ha'f so many teeth!

          Wall, we got to go to work.
          We see you later, Poppa.

DOUG: Hold on there, Antoine.
       We got work right here.

ANTOINE: You boys can't do it.
          You mighten hurt your hands
          den we all be outta work.

205

Nah, we got our saw and dat's enauf,
only maybe we just take dis whiskey bottle here
and call it resteetution.

[ANTOINE *picks up a whiskey bottle that is sitting on the sink.*]

What you t'ink 'bout dat, Poppa?

Wall, we caum back soon
haf another visit wi' da baby.

[*The three leave the shack with the saw and bottle.*
They walk and drink.
Suddenly, there is a young woman, an angel,
in a white waitress' uniform, standing in the road
in front of them, her hands outstretched and up,
palms turned in: the gesture of a blessing.]

ANGEL: The Lord be with you.

DOUG and ANTOINE: [*automatically*] And with thy spirit.

ANGEL: Behold! Be not afraid.
I have been sent to you.
I have good news for you.

DOUG: Sure you do and I suppose you come COD.

ANTOINE: Zip up dere Doug. Let'er talk.

ANGEL: Thanks, Frenchie. You boys don't remember me?
I'm the new one what's workin' nights
down to the Come and Eat.

ANTOINE: I t'ink I seen you in dere once or twice.

206

TOMMY: [*gawking*] Not me, man, I never see you in my life before.

DOUG: Okay, now you seen her. Let's go.
We got work to do.

ANGEL: Wait. Please. I ain't out here for my health, ya know.
I got to do this. You think I'd come out here,
freeze my butt, if I didn't have to?
I'm doin' it because he wants me to. I'm doin' it for him.

DOUG: Who?

ANGEL: The old guy.

DOUG: Huh?

ANGEL: Okay. I been workin' nights
down to the Come and Eat, like I said.
Things is always pretty slow, but I like it.
Gives me time to think. I like thinkin'.
And it gives me time to listen to the records.
I like that too.
There ain't much to do at that time of night.
I like it that way. The tips aren't great
'cause I ain't busy, but those that do come in
tip better than the ones during the day, besides
what the hell, I like bein' up all night
when everybody else is sleepin'. Sit around, ya know,
drink coffee, once in awhile get visitin' with a trucker.
It's nice, especially this time of year. It's cozy in there.
We got the Christmas lights all strung along the windows
and there's a wreath on the door and a little brush
on the windowsills. It's warm and nice in there
this time of year.

Anyway. This mornin' about four, I guess it was,

the door swings open and this big gust of snow
comes blowin' in and right behind it comes this old guy.
He must be eighty if he's a day.
He's got this great big overcoat what hangs down so far
it's draggin' on the floor and he's got on a flyer's hat,
that old fashioned kind, ya know?
The kind Snoopy wears
when he flies his doghouse.
I mean, this guy is a real sight.

He's a big guy and tall. Well, he's really skinny,
but he looks big in that coat. He's not fat at all,
and I can see he was damn good-lookin' once.
He's lanky. It takes him about two steps
to get across the place.

ANTOINE: Dat soun' like Uncle Forrest.

DOUG: Couldn't be. Forrest been dead for years.

ANTOINE: I know dat.
　　　　What you t'ink I don't know dat he been dead fer . . .

ANGEL: Hold it, Frenchie. I'm the one who's talkin'.
　　　　Besides, it wasn't whoever that is you're talkin' about.
　　　　This guy said his name was John. John Baptiste.

ANTOINE: Oh yeah?

ANGEL: Anyway, he sits down on a stool
　　　　at the counter and lets out this great big sigh
　　　　like he's all wore out or pissed off or somethin'.

　　　　Coffee, he says, so I get him a coffee.
　　　　Then he starts talkin' to me real nice and askin' me
　　　　all kinds of different questions, about myself, ya know,

208

real nice like. And he's smooth. I mean, fifty years ago
this guy mus'ta been somethin' else. I mean,
he was so nice.

So. Pretty soon I'm sittin' on the stool next to him
fillin' up his cup as fast as he can drink, and, God,
I guess I was, I'm just starin' him in the face
and we're talkin' and laughin'. . . .
I mean fifty years ago . . . oh, Jesus.

Then all of a sudden he gets real serious
and reaches over and takes my hand, and his hand
is bony and it's still cold, and he says real quiet
and real intense:
You have been called. You are the one.
You are the one to bring the news.

Well, I ought ta figure this guy is fuckin' crazy,
but I don't. He's got me sort of hypnotized or somethin';
I don't know. I guess . . . I mean . . . I liked him.
I *really* liked him, and he didn't scare me, not at all.

So he tells me to get out my pad and write down
what he tells me I got to say, and I do.
I got it right here. Then he tells me to come out here
and read all this stuff to you.
And that's why I'm here.

Is that wild or what? I know it sounds crazy,
but that's what really happened. I mean, I think it is.
I mean, he was really there, right there in the restaurant.
I mean, I think he was.

Sure he was. I seen him. I talked to him.
I poured him coffee.

Aw, hell! What difference does it make?
I'm here ain't I?

And I'm gonna do it like he told me to,
so gimme a break, okay?

I'm gonna start again.
And don't interrupt!

Okay. Here goes.

Behold! Be not afraid.
I have been sent to you.
I have good news for you.

And so it was that while they were there
the days were accomplished that she should be delivered.
And she brought forth her firstborn son
and wrapped him in a dirty old blanket
and laid him on a dirty old bed
inside a broken-down shack
because that is where they lived.

And nearby there were pulp cutters
walking down the road and drinking
and the angel of the Lord—
that's me—
the angel of the Lord came to them
and the glory of the Lord shone 'round about them
and they was sore afraid.

Then the angel of the Lord said to them:

I bring you good news of great joy
which shall be to *all* people,
for unto you is born this day a Savior
who is Christ the Lord.
And he will say to you:

The spirit of the Lord is upon me, because
He has anointed me to preach good news to the poor.

He has sent me to proclaim release to the captives
and recovering of sight to the blind
and to set at liberty all those who are oppressed.

And here is a sign for you. You will find the babe
wrapped in a blanket, lying on a bed,
beneath that star.

Joy to the world!
Glory to God in the highest!
Peace and Justice and Good Will
to everybody!
Go now and be with him.

[*The* ANGEL *disappears.* ANTOINE *and* DOUG *look to the star
and begin moving toward it, then realize that* TOMMY
is not with them. They go back.]

ANTOINE: Tommy? You ain't caumin' wid us?

DOUG: Com'on, kid, come with us.

TOMMY: You know where that star is.
          It's shinin' down on Arnie's house.

DOUG: I guess it is.

TOMMY: I ain't goin'.

DOUG: [*quietly*] Tommy, we're goin' to see the *baby*.
          He can't help who he got for a father.
          If people judged you by your folks, you'd be
          shit-out-of-luck, now wouldn't ya?

          Com'on, kid, come with us. You know you want to.

TOMMY: I can't go with you. I don't believe it.
Things just don't happen this way.

DOUG: Maybe not. But let's go see. Let's just go see.
We got nuthin' to lose, Tommy, nuthin'. Com'on.

[DOUG *puts his arm around* TOMMY.]

Open up that bottle, Antoine!
We got to get this boy here feelin' good.
And I'll have another go-round too.
Let's have another drink; then we'll get some presents
and go over there and have a visit.

ANTOINE: Yas, Tommy, here.
Slug it good.

TOMMY: But what about our work?

DOUG: Oh, Tommy, stuff the work.
You don't like it anyway.
Com'on!

[*The three start off toward the car.*]

Stuffit.
Stuff the goddamn crawler!
Stuff the goddamn saw!

Stick a peavey up your ass
and pray for an early thaw!

TOMMY: That ain't bad, Doug. Ain't bad.

Man, you see that pair of thirty-eights?

DOUG: She wan't wearin' pistols, was she?
I didn't see no pistols, you Antoine?

ANTOINE: Naow! But dat don't make no difference
to our Tommy boy.
I bet he still haffin' versions 'baout
how he got one in each hand.

TOMMY: Jeeze, you two are loonies.
You know, if I stay workin' with the both of you,
I'll get like that. I'm gonna get like you.
I will! I got to find another job.

ANTOINE: Bah! you stay wid us.
We all be rich, maybe tomorrow.
An' if we don't, dan we be lucky 'cause
we still haf' our reason why
we godda get our asses outta bed.

DOUG: Tommy got his reason why he godda keep his ass
into the bed! Oh, god! You are so lucky, Tommy.

TOMMY: I know I am. I know it, Doug. I know.

DOUG: Ah, stuff it!

And I bet he does too!
Go to it, boy! It's a hard job, Tommy,
but somebody's got to do it.
You be the one. Go to it, Tommy.

Oh, shit, you are so lucky!

Stuff it! And
Stuff the goddamn crawler
Stuff the goddamn saw.

TOMMY: I don't deserve this. I'm too young.

ANTOINE: Ain't nobody what deserve anyt'ing.

> If you be rich, you don't deserve it.
> If you be poor, you don't deserve dat needer.
> Pass on dat bottle.

DOUG: Stick a peavey up yer ass
    an' pray for an early thaw.

[ANTOINE *sings to the melody of the carol:* "*We Three Kings.*"]

ANTOINE: We t'ree kings ada puckerbrush are
    cuttin' pulp, ea-tin' caviar.
    Is it today, or is it tomorrow?
    Where da hell iss dat star?

TOMMY: I'm too young for this. I'm too young.

[The star shines down on GIL *and* ARNIE'S *shack.*
It floods the interior with light.
*Mary—*GIL*—is in bed with Jesus.*
*Joseph—*ARNIE*—stands to one side and to the other,*
the waitress—the attending ANGEL.

The pulp cutters reappear on the road near the shack.
Now in addition to the saw and bottle,
they have presents for the baby.
ANTOINE *has a toy chain saw;*
DOUG, *a leg of lamb and a sheepskin;*
TOMMY, *a baseball glove—a catcher's mitt.*

To the melody of "We Three Kings . . ."
the three together sing:]

ALL THREE: We are woodchucks through and through.
We draw pulp, unemployment too.
We get drunk and we get dirty
and we also chew.

Oh, we got nauthin', never had.
People think we're worthless, sad,
but, by Jesus, the angel pleased us
and we know we ain't all bad.

We three kings of Judevine are,
bearing gifts we brought from the car.
Swamp and back road, with our sack load,
following that there star.

Oh, we got nauthin', never had,
but ya know we ain't too bad.
We are brothers, got each other,
and the babe, the newborn lad.

ANTOINE: Dis here chain saw iss awful small,
but den again da baby ain't tall.
Whan he get bigger, dis be da rig fer
him make da tree to fall.

DOUG: A leg of lamb, a sheepskin rug,
these are the presents what come from Doug.
One's for the parents, one's for the baby,
and I may throw in a hug.

TOMMY: I will give this catcher's mitt.
I love this glove; it's a perfect fit.
Many a game we've played well together;
now to the babe I give it.

ALL THREE: Glorious now behold him arise,
King and God and Sacrifice;
Alleluia, Alleluia!
Sounds through the trees and skies.

Oh, we got nauthin', never had;
but we ain't useless, we ain't sad;
oh, by Jesus, the angel pleased us,
and we know we ain't too bad.

Alleluia, Alleluia!
We ain't useless; we ain't sad.
Alleluia, Alleluia!
Jesus Christ, we ain't too bad.
Alleluia, Alleluia!
Let's go see the newborn lad.

[*They step up to the shack.*
The ANGEL *greets them at the door.*
They approach the bed, the mother and the baby.]

ANTOINE: Wall, dis ain't be much. Got it down to
da discount store, but maybe it be saumt'ing
dat he like. Be just like da one his Poppa got.
See, you pull da cord, it go rum-rumrum.
I hope da little skipper like it.

[ANTOINE *leaves the toy saw on the bed and steps back.*]

DOUG: My wife and I boochered a lamb last night.
We figured you could use this leg, and this here skin
would make a nice rug for the baby.

[DOUG *places the leg of lamb and the skin on the bed*
and backs away.]

216

TOMMY: This ain't much of a present either,
           but, Jesus, I had some fun with it.
           It's a catcher's mitt, ya see?
           It's yours now.
           You hunker down behind the plate, like this.

           And you say, Chuckachucka. Pitchadamitt.
           Com'on, baby, Pitchadamitt.

[DOUG *pretends to pitch.* TOMMY *throws the ball back,*
  pounds on his glove and says again:]

           Chuckachucka. Pitchadamitt.
           Com'on, baby, Pitchadamitt.

           Well, I hope you have some fun.

[TOMMY *puts the mitt on the bed.*
  He looks down at the child and says:]

           Oh! Sweet babe, be careful what you do!
           This world is tough; it just ain't built
           for all the love you got.
           I fear for you!

           Aw, Jesus Christ!
           A man like you was shot!

                [*Tableau vivant*]

✦ ✦ ✦

WHAT I HEARD AT ROY MCINNES'

I was down to Roy McInnes' welding shop one other time
that winter Antoine, Doug and Tommy
worked together in the woods.

Guy Desjardins stopped in that time too. I think Guy
stopped in every time he passed through town just to warm
himself, have a cup of coffee, and say hello.

Guy hopped down out of the cab and immediately began
that little wintertime dance we all do
where you exhale rapidly and hop
back and forth from foot to foot while you pat your hands and say:
Jesus! Roy, is it cold enough for ya?

I can't remember what Roy said to that
but you're supposed to think of something funny.

Guy said "Hi" to me and I said "Hi" to him and we all
gathered around Roy's quadruple-chamber oil-drum stove.

Guy and Roy began to talk, and I began to listen.

Where you workin' now, Guy?

I'm drawing logs and pulp off the landing
up to where Antoine and Doug are cuttin',
the old Mead place, on the other side of Bear Swamp.
You know the place?

Well I guess I do. My grandmother
lived up there when she was just a little girl
before all us McInneses came down off the mountain
and settled down here in the village and got civilized.

They did, did they?
How come it never took with you?

I've wondered that myself.
Speakin' of wild ones, is that Stames boy
still workin' with those loonies?

Yes sir, he still is.
He's been workin' with them steady
since early this past fall.

Huh. He's stuck with them that long.

Yes sir.

It may be that that boy is settlin' down.

Well, you know. He's got himself a little family now.
What with Grace and the kids and all that kind of thing.
I think it gives him something to look forward to,
something to go to work for,
and, Jesus Christ, you know
a woman's good for any man.

No. I didn't know.

TOMMY AGAIN FINALLY

Antoine, Doug and Tommy cut logs and pulp right through that
    winter and into the spring.
When the black flies came out they gave up working in the woods,
and each went his separate way, found summer jobs,
or no jobs at all.

Tommy went on living with Grace and they both seemed happy as
   far as anybody could tell and Grace's kids did too.

I saw Grace down to Jerry's once that next spring and she had a
   pretty bad shiner,
but nobody said anything about it, and what people thought,
if anything, I can't say.

Then it was summer, the middle of July,
and Doug came through the door at Jerry's:

Tommy Stames shot himself.

What? What? What'd you say?

Tommy Stames killed himself.

What'd you say?

He shot himself up to his camp.

Where? Up to his camp?

Up to his camp. Antoine came and got me.

Tommy Stames killed himself. He shot himself.

Where?

He killed himself. Up to his camp.

Antoine came and got me. He left Antoine a note.
All it said was: Thank you, Antoine.
You know where to find me.

He shot himself?

Antoine came and got me. We went up.
We . . . we brought him back. He knew.

Tommy killed hisself. He killed hisself.

Tommy went up to his favorite place,
that little clearing in the woods.
He had a little camp up there, a fireplace,
a little lean-to made of spruce poles and
hemlock boughs. Why,
he camped up there.

And in the lean-to
there was a book of ancient Chinese poetry
and a Chinese painting
one of those long skinny ones
that start down close
and go up way up far
up into the mountains
and way up in the mountains in that painting
there was a little place
the Chinese called them pavilions
but it was just a lean-to
and a man sitting out in front of it,
just a tiny spot,
all alone
way up in the mountains.
Just like Tommy's place
and just like Tommy.

You go up through the woods and you cross a little stream
and you come to this clearing in the forest
where the light comes in.

Before he killed himself
he made a circle out of stones he'd gathered from the stream

and in the circle there were bits of bark and twigs,
little signs or symbols,
something.

You go up through the woods and cross a little stream.

Antoine came and got me. We went up. We brought him back.

A clearing in the forest where the light comes in.

He camped up there.
It was a little lean-to in the forest.

He put himself in the middle of that circle.
He was sitting down.
He took his army carbine. . . .

You go up through the woods.

He left a note for Antoine.

You cross a little stream.

A clearing in the forest.

And he shot himself right through the heart.
He knew exactly where his heart was at.
He didn't miss.
He fell backward on the ground. He was laid out on the ground.
Like Jesus on the cross,
with his arms spread out.
He died right away and right inside that stone circle
he had made with the pebbles from the stream.

You could tell he didn't suffer.
He looked so peaceful, like he felt good . . .

like he . . . finally . . . felt good.

In the forest where the light comes in.

And on his shirt he had pinned
a little piece of paper
and on it he had written:

Grace and Peace be with Me.

GRACE SPEAKS

Not long after Tommy died, I saw Grace
down in the village one day.

Hi, Grace. Hi. I'm . . .
I'm sorry.

I don't want your sympathy.
I don't want to talk to you
or anybody else around here either.

I heard what Edith said about Tommy bein'
a stick of dynamite ready to go off in somebody's face.
Well, she was right, wasn't she? Only thing that she got wrong
was whose face it was gonna be.

Maybe it's better. I mean, folks like Tommy and me,
we don't have much future anyway. Isn't that right?
It's all uphill for us, you know?
Everything's against us from the start.

It's the people around here drove him to it.
They had him all figured out, didn't they?

They didn't want to listen to anything except
what makes 'em feel all warm and gooey
or righteous or somethin'.
Nobody ever wants to listen to the truth!
Nobody ever wants to know what Tommy
thinks and feels!

You know, you and your kind can keep this up only so long.
You can't keep us down forever, one day
we are going to. . . . How—can you tell me how?—
are my kids ever gonna get anything better 'an what I got!
How they ever gonna . . . They got to live! . . .

We are going to be your servants and your slaves
only a little while longer,
and then we are going to rise up and swarm all over you
like spiders, like napalm!
I am warning you! I'm warning you!

Grace, I'm not one of . . .

You're not one of them? You got land, don't ya?
You live up there on the hill, don't ya?
You inherit some money so you could buy that land?

Well, I . . .

I knew you did. I knew you did.
You know what I inherited?
A kitchen table, with the Formica already worn off.

You keep sayin' how you want to give me my chance,
how you want to stand up for me. You don't.
I know you don't. You don't give a shit for me, David.

No, Grace.

You look at me and you don't even see me.
All you see is what you want to see.
I am invisible to you.

No! That isn't true!

You know what I would like to do?
I'd like to tear out both your eyes!
Then maybe you could see me!

Well, I'm doin' houses now. I mean, in addition
to working down to Stowe.
Maybe I could do your house for you.
Call me if you want to.

PART IV

THE FIRE BURNS BRIGHTER THE DARKER IT GETS

I

Raymond pulled three large, delicately orange and cylindrical
    carrots
out of the garden soil, wiped the damp earth from their sides,
wiped his hands on his overalls and strode, loping his long and
    easy strides,
out of the garden and across the driveway and dooryard
to the woodshed and the rain barrel at the corner of the
    woodshed
where he plunged the three carrots, their tops still on them,
into the shaded and cool fifty-five-gallon drum of water.

He drenched them a few times, then held them out and shook
    them the way you shake down a thermometer.

He put the carrots on a shelf attached to the woodshed wall next
    to and just above the rain barrel,
took down the rubber basin that hung on a nail above the shelf
    and dipped it into the water.
He put the basin on the shelf and washed his hands, lathering
    them with soap, then scrubbing the dirt out from under his
    fingernails with a small brush.
He threw the basinful of soapy water across the lawn and dipped
    out another basin of water and this time
washed his face and splashed water on his hair.
He threw this second basin of water across the lawn also,
dipped into the rain barrel for a third, swilled the water around in
    the basin and threw it across the lawn as well.

He hung the basin back on its nail on the woodshed wall and took
    down the towel which hung next to the basin on another nail.
He dried his hands and face and hair and put the towel back
    where it stayed.

He took a comb from the shelf and combed his white hair while
    watching himself in a small, rectangular mirror, the silver
    backing on which was bubbled and browned in the lower left
    hand corner.

Raymond took hold of the carrots which were lying on the shelf,
and stepped around the corner of the woodshed.
He paused on the dooryard lawn momentarily,
saw the blue sky, the white clouds, the big, hazy-vague spine of
    mountains thirty miles to the west,
his luxuriant and bountiful late summer garden, his dooryard and
    his little house.
He smelled August and the smell of his own sweat and sunburned
    flesh.
He loved the way he smelled, the way he stank.
It was the odor of honest, human labor under the summer sun and
    in the summer earth,
as distinct and pleasing a smell
as that of a lathered horse or a transpiring stand of balsam on a
    sultry summer day, or
a freshly pulled carrot.

He listened to the few birds who sang at that moment and to a
    small breeze
as it moved across the lawn, through the dooryard apple tree and
    away.
He mounted the porch steps, and entered into the porch's shade,
walked to the far end of the porch, sat down on the suspended
    swing, pushing it a little more than a little as he sat down,
and began rocking.

He put two of the carrots beside him on the seat, put the third in
    his mouth,
held it firmly between his teeth and puffed on the carrot as if it
    were a cigar.

He smiled to himself and remembered back thirty years to the last
  time he had smoked a real cigar,
and his remembering brought him to a reverie of those years so
  long ago
when he and Ann were young and strong and filled with the juice
of life.

Tears wet his face, blurred his vision. He moved his body
back and forth in keeping with the steady cadence of the swing.
He rocked and cried. Then

he bit into the carrot suddenly and forcefully.
It gave way under the pressure of his jaws with a crisp pop.
He was almost seventy years old and alone in the world, in this
  place where just two years ago he had not been alone. Yet,
he could eat a carrot.

He reached into the right-hand, rear pocket of his overalls and
  took out his bandana,
wiped his face and dried his eyes and then blew his nose hard into
  his bandana again and again, each time honking loud enough
to startle the ducks lounging in the sun on the edge of the pond
  below the garden.
He wiped his nose and jammed the wet bandana back into the
  big, right-rear pocket of his overalls.

He could eat a carrot. He had his teeth, his own teeth, and they
  were still firm and strong, as were his jaws.
And, although eating a carrot while sitting on his own porch
  swing on a summer day while watching his own garden and the
  mountains beyond
was not solace for the loneliness and grief he felt, it was not
  without its pleasures.

He bit again into the carrot, coming down hard on the firmness of

its flesh, severing it from its green top.
He smiled to himself and was proud, vainly proud, of his strong
  teeth and firm gums.
He looked out at the mountains and he chewed and smiled
and ate all the carrots and he was alone and lonely
and almost unbearably sad and happy.
And the carrots tasted good.

II

Raymond heard a car slowing down on the road below the house,
then turning and coming up the lane and into view.

It was Sarah.

It had been ten years since Sarah and Timothy arrived in Judevine
  and adopted Raymond and Ann as surrogate parents.
When Sarah and Timothy broke up, Raymond and Ann grieved
  as any parents would,
and when Sarah embarked upon a series of brief partnerships with
  numerous men, Raymond and Ann worried.
When Breeze Anstey arrived and Breeze and Sarah established
  their herb farm, Raymond and Ann rejoiced in the hope that
  finally perhaps some stability might come to Sarah's life.
Raymond wondered privately during those days whether the two
  young women were lovers as well as friends,
and his wondering made him feel restless and dissatisfied with the
  regularity and commonness of his own life.
After Breeze Anstey left, the closeness between Raymond and
  Ann and Sarah waned, and they saw less and less of her.

Yet, two summers ago when Ann died, Sarah came to the house
  and grieved with the other few neighbors,
and when the others forgot about Raymond and his loneliness, as
  people always do, Sarah did not forget.
She continued to stop by, not so often as to make a nuisance of

herself but often enough to let Raymond know she was thinking of him.

And she brought fresh bread she'd made or beer from town and they would drink together and visit.

She also sometimes called Raymond on the telephone in the evenings just to say hello and to see how he was doing.

Her calls and her visits were more sustenance to Raymond than her bread and he was appreciative and full of thanks.

So, when he saw that it was Sarah come for a visit on such a summer afternoon, he smiled broadly and his heart beat faster

and he roused himself out of the swing and went to the porch steps to greet her.

Sarah got out of the car, reached back in for a six-pack of beer, turned and headed up the dooryard lawn toward the porch.

Hi.

Hi.

Nice day.

Sure is.

Come on up and sit down.

Thank you.

Sarah put the six-pack down on the porch railing, and without asking if he wanted one,

she opened a beer and handed it to him, then opened one for herself.

Raymond took the bottle from her with his left hand and with his right picked up the carton of beers from the sunny railing and

placed it at the back of the porch in the shade.
Sarah and Raymond both moved to the swing where they sat
   down together
and in silence began to drink.

Raymond and Sarah sat for a long time drinking the cold beer and
   moving back and forth on the swing and watching out across
   the dooryard lawn, across the garden to the mountains.
Then Raymond opened his mouth
and let go a long, deep, loud, resonant belch.

Good, Raymond said.

Yeah, Sarah said.

After a short time, Sarah prepared herself, opened her mouth and
   also belched.

Raymond turned and looked at her.

Good, Sarah said.

Yeah, Raymond said.

And all this time they kept swinging and rocking and not looking
   at each other, except that once,
but rather looking straight ahead out across the garden and the
pond.

Raymond finished his beer first and with a thrusting motion
he propelled the swing forward making it move a little faster,
in a wider arc, so that he could reach out, stretching his arm out,
as the swing swung forward, and lightly set the empty beer bottle
down on the railing. Then he relaxed into the swing again and let

the swing lessen its arc and slow to a quieter, easier rocking
back and forth.

He put his hands on the seat of the swing, palms down and fingers
    spread,
and he paid attention to the rocking of the swing and to the slight
    feeling of euphoria
that one beer on a hot summer afternoon had given him.
He felt light and airy, flexible and smooth.

You've never gotten used to it, have you? Sarah asked.
I mean a day like today.

No. Not a day like today.

Then they were silent again for a time.

You're taking such good care of yourself,
and this place looks great too.

Did you think I wouldn't?

Well, no . . . I just thought . . .

You just thought I'd be helpless . . .
one of those men who can't survive without a woman.

Yes . . . that's exactly what I thought.

It's been two years, you know. I miss her still, terribly, but
I want to live. I get along okay. I'm glad to see the morning come.
I've got my health and I'm happy to have another day.

So you're not really all that lonely.

I'm very lonely. But that's just the way things are.

I envy you, Raymond.

Sarah reached over with her right hand and touched Raymond's
calloused and strong left hand which lay now relaxed and on its
back on the seat of the swing, the palm up and open
and the fingers curled in that arc of palm and fingers
that comes from a lifetime of holding tools.
Then she slid her hand onto his and wove her fingers between his
    fingers, and let her hand rest there.

So much of the time I feel so restless, dissatisfied. I get so sick of
    my place,
being trapped there all the time. All I can think about is getting
    out.
I promise myself, I'll go back to where I came from or someplace
    else,
but I never go, because just when I think I'm about to actually do
    it,
pack up and leave, something happens—like today, and I can't go,
I don't want to. I'm stuck here forever, and what's worse, I want
    to be.

Raymond hadn't heard a word Sarah had been saying.
All he could think about, all he could feel, was her hand in his.

Abruptly and with one motion Raymond stopped the swing with
    his foot, pulled his hand away from hers and got up,
leaving the swing and Sarah to wobble awkwardly from side to
    side.

I can't stand it when you touch me. I'm sorry, Sarah, but . . .
oh, you must think I'm some kind of odd duck, but
I can't stand it!

I'm sorry.

It's not your fault. I love it when you do, but I can't stand it.

I didn't mean to upset you. It's just so nice to be here with you,
to touch you.

Yes, it is! I mean . . . when you do. That's why I can't stand it.

I didn't mean anything by it.

I know you didn't.

Raymond, I'm sorry if I offended you or made you feel
uncomfortable.
I'm just glad to be here with you.

And I'm glad you're here.

I'm sorry.

Don't be.

Raymond moved about on the porch a little, pacing.

Sarah, I have to say something to you,
and I'm afraid you're going to laugh at me.

I won't.

You might.

I won't!

Sarah, this is hard enough for me without your getting angry.

I'm not angry.

You are.

I'm not!

Why are you so upset? What'd I do?

Nothing.

Is all this because I said you might laugh?

Yes.

All this over that?

Yes.

Jesus.

And about your not wanting me to touch you.

But, you said you didn't mean anything by it.

I lied. I did mean something. I like being here with you. I love it.
It feels warm and comfortable here. You're easy to talk to.
I feel relaxed here. And when I'm here with you, I'm not lonely.
I love it here . . . with you.

There were a few tears sliding down Sarah's face.

Raymond returned to the swing, sat down, reached toward Sarah
and with the backs of his fingers stroked her cheek as if to wipe
    away her tears.

Sarah took his hand in her hands and held it for a moment
    close to her nose and mouth.
Raymond could feel her warm breath.

Sarah sniffed and said:
You've been pulling carrots. I can smell the tops.
They smell nice—like Queen Anne's lace.

Then Sarah put Raymond's hand in her lap.

Raymond looked at his hand as it lay on the softness of her lap.
It seemed detached from his body, abandoned there,
as if it were a fledgling bird fallen from its nest and discovered in
    the grass and brought into the house where a woman cradled it
    gently while those with good intentions tried to decide what to
    do.
Raymond looked at the hand which seemed not to belong to
    him, yet through it he could feel the cotton of her skirt,
the firmness of the inside of her thighs.

He pulled his hand away from where it had been touching her
    body,
  stood up, turned his back to the yard and garden and faced Sarah.

I can't stand it when you touch me, because I'm in love with you.

The blood rose in Sarah's neck and flushed up into her face.
She looked straight at Raymond and said:
And I'm in love with you.

You can't be.

Why not?

I'm too old. You're too young.
Next year I'm seventy.

Next year I'm thirty-nine.

Half my age.

So?

Do you mean that?

Yes.

At night, Sarah . . . I lie in bed awake and I imagine that you are
    here with me,
that we are together working in the garden or the woods or in
    town shopping at the grocery or the feed store.
I imagine that you and I are here . . . together.

Raymond turned from Sarah again and stood near the porch steps.
Sarah rose and came to him, she pressed herself against him
and they wrapped their arms around each other.

I have that dream too.

They held each other quietly for a long time.
Then Raymond gently pushed her away.

I couldn't. I can't. She's still just too much with me. I'm sorry.

What's wrong with me?

It's not you! It's me! It's Annie! There's nothing wrong with you.

It *is* me! It's always me! What's wrong with me, Raymond!
I'm not even forty years old, I've been through half a dozen
relationships. Every one of them has failed! Why!
What's wrong with me !

Sarah moved down the porch steps and a little way across the
 lawn.
She sat down, put her head in her hands and began sobbing
 bitterly.

Raymond eased himself down onto the porch steps and listened to
 Sarah,
to the heaves and shivers, the sighs and moans of her anguish.
Slowly Sarah's weeping quieted and settled into a kind of steady,
 even sob and moan.

III

The angle of light had grown more and more acute as the
 afternoon began to give way to the evening.
The tree swallows and barn swallows and their litters of young
 swooped and twittered above and through the garden catching a
 late afternoon hatch of insects.
A couple of cows blatted in the near distance and in the far
 distance, off on the mountainside to the east, the faint sound of
 a chain saw came and went as the afternoon's wind shifted
 direction.
And there were other songs as well.

The *kuk-kuk-kutuck* of a pileated woodpecker just beyond the

pond, in his or her usual place, off into the woods, the same
   place year after year.
The guttural stammer of the ravens who lived in the eastward
   mountains and who daily came over Raymond's house to see
   what he had done, how things had changed from the day
   before.
The shrill whistle of some kind of a hawk so high above the
   house it was invisible.

And there were the calls of the smaller, closer, more familiar
   summer birds.
The white-throated sparrow's eleven-note song saying:
   old Sam Pea-bo-dy, Pea-bo-dy, Pea-bo-dy.
The similar three- and five-note songs of the chickadee who sang:
dee-dee-dee, chick-a-dee-dee-dee; dee-dee-dee, chick-a-dee-dee.
The gurgle of the yellowthroat down in the wet place beside the
   pond.
The cluck of a robin.
The odd and beautiful lowing squeak of the cedar waxwing.
And down across the road in the pasture, the salubrious warble of
   the bobolink—this bird of the broadening fields who never
   came near the house since it was too close to the woods for this
   singer of the open spaces.
And added to these songs just now was Sarah's song,
   her sad and beautiful weeping, this song of the anguish of her life.

And beneath and among and above all this, always and constantly,
   the late summer hum of insects, billions and billions of insects,
all making their own individual species sound, all crying, singing
   and crying their way toward their fall graves.

And thrown over this cornucopia of sound,
as if it were a soft, translucent veil:
the ever-present and delicate silence of the wilderness.

IV

Raymond stood up and went to where Sarah was sitting.
He eased himself down on the lawn beside her, reached up under
    her long hair and caressed the back of her neck.
She rolled toward him and sadly put her head on his shoulder.

I'm sorry, Sarah.

Me too.

This whole thing. . . it scares me. I'm afraid of it.

I am too.

But not as much as me.

You don't know that.

You've been through all this more than once before.
I never have. I lived my whole life with just one woman.

And that's why this has got to scare me just as much as it scares
    you.
I've been through it over and over again and every time it fails,
I fail, it falls apart, and I'm alone again. Don't you think
that would make me just as afraid as you?

Yes, I do.

More afraid. All I've ever known is failure.
All you've ever known's success.

I wouldn't call it that.

I want what you and Annie had. I've always wanted that.

I want that too, again. But I need time . . . to forget.
It always happens that way. I mean, eventually, we forget.

Sarah moved closer to Raymond and put her arms around him.

I know. My mother's only been dead ten years, and already
I can barely remember her. I try to bring her back, see
the two of us together in some memory, remember the details,
    just how she was, how she looked and acted, just exactly the
    sound of her voice, how she walked, what it felt like to touch
    her,
and I can't. I can't remember. She's gone.

And then the dead are really dead.

Yes.

For me, Sarah, that time isn't yet, but I want to also tell you this.
I'm on fire for you, and the fire burns brighter the darker it gets.

Then what are we going to do about it?

Nothing.

Why?

Because I'm not ready. I'm afraid.

I'm afraid too, Raymond, but I'm also unhappy and lonely and it
    seems like I have always been.
I want my life to change! I know you need time,
but I don't have it. I can't wait. I'm alone again.

I don't want to be alone.
I'm going home.

Don't.

I have got to.

Why?

Because I can't stand this any longer!
It's all too much for me! It's too painful.

Will you come see me again?

I don't know. I don't think so. No. This is too hard for me.

What are you going to do?

I'm going to go home and do what I've been doing most of my
   life. I'm going to be alone.

Sarah sniffed, wiped her eyes, got up and brushed off her skirt:

I'm sorry, Raymond, but I just can't stand this.

Come see me again.

No. I can't.

Please.

No. When you're ready, you come see me.
Maybe I'll still be around.

Sarah walked to her car, got in, started the engine and drove off.
She didn't look back, she didn't wave.

Raymond stood on the lawn and watched her leave.
Then he headed for the barn to begin his evening chores.
He didn't feel like supper.

About half way to the barn, Raymond stopped, turned, looked at
    his house, at the swing on the porch, at the lawn
where he and Sarah had been sitting,
then he turned his face to the heavens and said:

Annie! It's not fair!

✦ ✦ ✦

HOW I CAME TO GET THE POEMS
THAT TOMMY WROTE FOR GRACE

It was more than a year after Tommy died.
The phone rang one morning; it was Grace:

I want to apologize for the way I spoke to you
the last time we saw each other. I'm sorry.
I was wondering if I could come up, just for a second.
I've got something I'd like to show you.

I said sure and she hung up.

I was shocked and curious and anxious and excited
by her forwardness, her reaching out to me. It wasn't like her,
or anyone else in these parts. I waited by the window
watching for her car. Then I saw it down on the road
slowing to make the turn into the drive and up to the house.
She got out of the car, reached back in to get a large, manila,
clasp-type envelope, closed the door, turned
and moved up the sloping lawn toward the house cradling the
    envelope in her arms and pressing it against her breasts the way
    schoolgirls carry their books.

I was waiting on the porch.
She looked directly at me, smiled and said: Hi.

I said Hi and something about the clarity and warmth and color of
    the day,
and Grace nodded as if to tell me she didn't want to go through all
    that bullshit socializing.

I'm sorry to bother you. I could have sent you these,
but I wanted to hand them to you face-to-face. It's not easy.
I know we've had our differences, but I. . . .

I broke in and said how pleased and flattered I was that she'd
    come,
and then, although I began to stumble, I started saying how I
    knew
how hard it was to reach out and how hard it must be for her
    right now.

Thank you, but I don't need your help, and I don't want
your explanations either. I came up here to give you these
and to tell you why I wanted to.
Just give me a chance, will you please?
I'm sorry. But I said it wasn't easy.

Grace cast down her eyes. She seemed defeated.

Would you like some coffee?

She raised her head and looked at me again.

Yes. That would be nice. Thank you.

In her eyes there was an intensity of stare,
a depth of rage and pain and a warm affection
that made me shudder.

I went inside and left Grace sitting in a lawn chair on the porch.
I came back with a pot of coffee on a tray, two mugs, two spoons,
    sugar, half-and-half and a few pieces of anisette toast on a small
    plate.
I set it down on the overturned wooden box we used for a coffee
    table and poured.

This is nice. Thank you.

She smiled at me again, then fixed her coffee and settled back into
   her chair.

I know we've had our differences
and in lots of ways I still think
you are a royal asshole,
but being a poet and all, well,
I thought maybe you would understand,
besides, I mean,
who else could I turn to?

No offense intended, but
you're the best that I can do.

What's in this envelope is Tommy's poems,
I mean the ones he wrote for me.
I wanted to share them, wanted to
show them to somebody.

Huh. Probably now you too will think what Edith,
and everybody else around here says is true,
probably you'll think I'm pretty kinky,
being as, you'll see, they are mostly pretty sexy.

But I thought I'd bring them to you anyway.
I mean, I think they're good.
And I thought maybe—someday
you could put them in a book.

◆

In the manila envelope Grace brought me,
   there were fifty-four poems in what seemed to me a roughly
   chronological order—
from their first ecstatic encounters, through a period of calm,

into a time of disillusionment and depression,
to the final disaster that befell them,
in other words, giving, as all real poems do,
the news of their lives.

I have selected thirteen of the fifty-four.

OH!

THIRTEEN POEMS

by Tommy Stames

LOVER, STRANGER, FRIEND

How can it be?
Just a year ago
I didn't even know
your name, I
had never seen
your face.

What or who
let us know each other
in this way?
What or who
has blessed us,
given us
this peace?

Lover, stranger, friend,
this nakedness I have with you—
it is a balm, a gift
to soothe
my wounded life,
my loneliness.

MORNING POEM

She gets out of bed and moves
to the windows where she drops
her nightgown to the floor
then stands naked
in the early morning light
looking out the window.

He lies in bed and watches her.

He is warm under the covers.
Early summer. Six A.M.

His eyes touch the inside of her thighs,
her hairy mound; they part her lips;
they dance across her body.

She steps into her underpants
and pulls them up.

Both she and the room are chilled
and her nipples are standing up.
Her areolas are dark and rough.

She bends over slightly,
settles her breasts into her bra,
then stands up and hitches it
behind her. Her nipples
press against the fabric.

She pulls a cotton turtleneck
down over her chest. Still
he can see the hard points
of her nipples through her shirt.

She steps into her jeans.
He hears, he sees the snap,
the zipper going up.

He hears her naked feet
across the floor
headed for the coffee.

253

We are standing together,
your back to me,
my arms around you,
like this:

my right hand inside
your underpants, my fingers
between your lips,
my other hand cupped
around your right breast
and lifting so that
your breast
is round
like a grapefruit,

your other breast resting
in the corner of my forearm,
my chin resting on your shoulder,
my eyes watching all of this,
and you leaning up against me.

I think about the miracle of the spirit
settled in the flesh, your soul abiding
in this body and I think about all this
because of what I touch and see:

The firmness of your breasts,
the hardness of your nipples,
the softness of your shoulder on my lips,
the delight I feel between my thighs,
the heat inside your mound which is
getting slippery, getting wet.

OH!

When I sit between
your legs and you
take your fingers,
part those lips and show
the inside of
the mound of my desire,

my eyes bug out,
my mouth drops open,
my hands go up,
palms out and fingers splayed
and I say:
Oh!

Just like a picture I saw once
of an old aboriginal man
sitting by a fire in the dark
telling a story to children,
his eyes bugged out,
his hands waving in the air,
his whole body gesturing:
Oh!

A FLEETING ANIMAL

When you abandon everything
and give yourself to me,
when I abandon everything
and give myself to you,
we make a fleeting animal
of such beauty, passion,
nakedness and grace
that I am glad it slips away
when we are done,
because this world is
hurt and cruel and nothing
that naive, loving and unashamed
could possibly survive.

THREE PARTICULAR INSTANCES
OF THE UNIVERSAL SOUL

The woman is naked and
stepping into the tub,
half of her has already disappeared
behind the shower curtain.
The man is standing at the sink
in his underpants shaving.
The child is sitting on the toilet
peeing, her pants and underpants
down around her ankles.
Her feet don't quite touch the floor.

The three of them are visiting
about some of the kids
in the child's class at school
or they are talking about
what they did yesterday
or what they will do today.

The universal soul has flaked off
three particular souls
who have come together
in this bathroom in a kind of oneness
which is an imitation of
the universal soul itself.

It is an imitation of heaven.

They bathe, shave, pee, talk,
they look at each others' nakedness,
and they know a kind of calm, delight,
an ease, in the presence of each other
which is ecstasy.

PRAISE FOR MY LIFE

The garden is free of weeds.
The vegetables blossom
and grow large.

This woman is beautiful
and gentle. Her children
are loving and kind.

In the cool of the evening
the kids and the dogs
romp and clown on the lawn
and the night birds begin to sing.

WAIT

I can see the sadness
of your life today.
It looks out
from behind your eyes.

You have turned
within yourself today
and wrapped yourself
around your wounded friend,
the one whose name is
Anger-Grief, the one
who looks out
from behind your eyes.

There is no touch
no kiss, no sigh
today
that can save you
from your pain.

I can see the sadness
of your life today.
I can see it in your eyes.

And tomorrow I will be
the one who moves across
our lives dancing with
my own wounded friend.

And tomorrow, will you,
please, be the one
who waits for me?

THE ANGEL OF DEPRESSION

The angel of depression
came today
and took my soul away.
She left my body
lying on this bed
curled in upon itself as if
I had not yet
been born.

The angel of depression
came today
and left me motionless,
lying still as death,
waiting here

until her brighter sister,
the one who looks like you,
comes to take me in her arms
and raise me up
and put her mouth on mine
and breathe back into me
my life.

When you take
my soul from me

where do you go with it
and what do you do
and why do you take it anyway
and how come I
can't protect myself
from you and why
once you've taken it
why do you let your
brighter sister bring it
back to me?

AFTER READING A POEM BY TU FU

In the coolness of the evening
I fell asleep and dreamed
that you were here and we
were joined together

and as you shivered
as you came
you softly
gently
spoke my name.

NOT MUCH

Union Oneness Ecstasy
is all I ever wanted.

LAST POEM

The angel of depression came today
and this time took both my body and
my soul away.

She told me to leave this note for you
to tell you that her brighter sister,
that's the one who looks like you,
will not be allowed to save me.

She says this time no one
will be allowed to save me.

The angel of depression came today
and this time she didn't only
take my soul away, this time
I went with her.

EXPLANATION

I made all these
so you would
fall in love with me.

REPRISE FOR TOMMY

I made a poem for you. You wanna hear it?
Sure.
Tommy Stames shot himself. He killed himself.

What? What did you say?

He shot himself. He killed himself.
Up to his camp.

You go through the woods and you cross a little stream.
It was a clearing in the forest
where the light comes in.

He had a little lean-to,
a fireplace,
a book of Chinese poetry.

And on his shirt he had pinned a little piece of paper.
And on it he had written:
Grace and Peace be with Me.

This never ending dream—
You sure got a nice place here, Joe—
of wilderness and freedom and bread.

I made a poem for you.
I made a poem for you.
Grace and Peace be with Me.

✦ ✦ ✦

RAYMOND AND SARAH AGAIN

I

It was almost exactly a year from the time Raymond and Sarah
    confessed their love for one another until they saw each other
    again.

How such things can happen, how two people who obviously
    have so much affection for each other
and who live less than two miles apart and who both could so
    much benefit from being with each other,
how they could go an entire year without seeing each other,
    without even bumping into each other
in town at a store or passing on the highway,
is such a mystery and so against the mathematics of probability
    or chance
that there has got to be some kind of deliberate if unconscious
    distancing mechanism operating,
as if they were like poles of two magnets so that whenever they
    began to come near each other they were pushed away
by that invisible field of energy that insured they would never
    see or touch each other,
 and all this no doubt because they had each frightened the other
    so completely in their encounter a year earlier
as to make necessary such a total and complete separation.

Yet an even larger mystery was what on earth made Sarah on this
    particular July day
defy the invisible field and get into her car and drive the scant
    two miles straight to Raymond's place
without even the slightest notion of an excuse for doing so,
drive determinedly and too fast into his driveway,
pull to a stop in the dooryard so abruptly that the car skidded on
    the gravel,
get out of her car and practically stomp toward the garden where
    Raymond was working, come up to him

267

as he stood where the corn ended and the beans began, and, planting her feet wide apart, then planting her hands on her hips, say:

I've come to see you.

I can see that.

That's the welcome I get?

It's been a whole year!

I know that.

You could have at least called.

You could have called me too!

Yes, I could have.

Why do I always have to be the one to initiate the contact!

You told me not to.

I didn't! All I said was I couldn't wait.

You said you'd never come see me again!

That's right! I did! So what?
You don't know how to use the telephone?
Why do I always have to be the one to reach out to you?
You could of called me just as easily as I could have called you!

I'm going to finish weeding these beans. Do you want to join me?

No! I want you to answer my questions!

Sarah, who was barefooted, turned on her heel so hard she
    literally screwed herself into the garden's soft earth a couple of
    inches.
Then she stomped off heading toward her car.

Raymond threw aside the hoe he had been leaning on and strode
    after her.
He had to run a little to catch her. When he did he took her
    elbow gently,
stopped her, turned her toward himself, and said:

Don't go, please.
Help me weed the beans.

I don't want to help you weed your goddamn beans.
I want to know why you let a whole year go by without even
    saying hello.

I didn't call you because I was afraid.
You said you would probably never come see me again,
and since you never did, I figured you didn't want to.
Why should I pursue someone who doesn't want me?
You were the one, you know you were, who rejected me.

Not entirely. You said no to me more than I said no to you.

Yes. That's true.

I practically begged you.

But you did say you'd never come see me again.

I had to recover somehow.

I was respecting your wishes.

You should have known.

I was afraid.

I'm here now.

I'm glad.

They walked back toward the rows of beans and bent to the task
    of weeding.
When they neared the end of the second row, Raymond stood up,
held his lower back, groaned, and said:

It's way past time for my dinner. Will you join me?

They went out of the garden and to the rain barrel at the edge
    of the woodshed
where they washed face and hands in the rubber basin,
dried themselves on the towel hanging on the woodshed wall
and went into the house.

II

What struck Sarah first upon entering the kitchen was what always
    struck her first:
the floor: the plain, unfinished rock maple floor.
In more than forty years there had never been any varnish or stain
    or wax applied to it—not ever,
only decades of sweeping with a broomstraw broom
which had polished the floor to a light beige, almost white,
    radiance,
a stunning patina: the strong, soft, natural glow of the naked wood
    slowly wearing away,

the same strong, natural glow, Sarah thought, that radiated from
    Raymond
as he wore away also.

It's cool and nice in here, Sarah said.

I drew the blinds.

There was a pot of soup simmering on the stove.
Raymond took bread from the bread box, a cutting board, a
    butcher knife. He took a pitcher of raw milk from the
    refrigerator, some glasses, some soup plates from the cupboard.
He brought the pot of soup to the table, served the two of them
and they ate.

Good soup.

Garden vegetable.

May I have some more?

I like that.

What?

You said may, not can.

Raymond took Sarah's soup plate from her and she watched him
    ladle the soup out of the pot.
She heard the little clank of the soup ladle against the bottom of
    the empty plate as he dished the first scoop in.

She ate two plates of soup, a couple of pieces of bread, drank a
    large glass of milk. He did the same.
When she was done she leaned back in her chair, slouched a little

and watched Raymond slurp the last of his soup out of his spoon.
She stared at him.

Sarah got up from her chair, came around to where Raymond was
    sitting, bent down and kissed him on the mouth,
then she stood up again and pressed his face against her breasts
and held his face there for a moment.

I'm always the one who starts it.

Yes.

Raymond stood up, took her hand and led her out of the kitchen,
across the living room and into the bedroom.

They stood next to the bed and he began unbuttoning her blouse.
When he reached her waist he pulled the blouse out from inside
the waistline of her skirt.

He touched her hair, her forehead, her ears, the closed lids of both
    eyes, the sides of her neck.
He touched her shoulders under her blouse, her armpits, her
    breasts, her belly, her navel.

Then Raymond stepped back, as if he'd forgotten something
or done something wrong, and began to undress himself, so that
he might be naked and exposed, before Sarah's nakedness
was uncovered.

He stood then embarrassed and shy in front of her
and she looked at his old and skinny and wounded body
with its erect penis pointing toward her.

Raymond came close to Sarah again, reached out and with the
    tips of the fingers on both hands,

pushed the blouse gently over her shoulders and let the blouse
    fall to the floor.
Sarah pushed her skirt down to her ankles and stepped out of it,
then did the same with her underpants.

The two of them stood apart for a time and looked at each other's
    wounds,
the imperfections, the big and little deformities,
at the ravages of aging,
his being so much more extensive than hers, yet hers
extensive enough also as they obliterated
the last vestiges of her youth.

They looked at these marks and scars, these histories of their
    bodies, these signs of the deepening pain of age,
and then they lay down together.

III

They were lying on their backs side by side,
Raymond with his hands behind his head,
Sarah with her hands up around her chin clutching the sheet to
    her neck,
when Raymond said:

It's difficult. I mean it's strange, new.

And disappointing . . . a let down.

It was for me too, you know.

I'm not arguing with you; I'm agreeing with you.
Don't expect so much so soon. We build up these things
in our imaginations until nothing could ever match the fantasy.

I was going to say that to you.

It's just a let down. It's not that big a deal, that's all.

Raymond wrapped his left arm around Sarah and drew her to
 himself.

I guess what we need is just a lot of practice.

Sarah chortled, poked Raymond in the ribs hard enough to make
 him jump, then cuddled herself into him
and lay her face on his breast. She fell asleep almost immediately
and her body twitched those tiny electric twitches of profound
 sleep and she snored a little and slobbered on Raymond's chest.
Raymond looked down at her and was amazed,
and then he fell asleep also.

IV

It's three o'clock! We've slept more than an hour.
I have tea at three.

Hot tea? In July?

Every day, no matter. Every day for forty-two years.
Hot tea at three.

Raymond got out of bed, dressed, and walked barefooted into the
 kitchen where he turned on the stove and set a kettle of water
 to boil.
When the water boiled and he had steeped a pot of tea under its
 cozy and gotten out mugs and cream and sugar,
he called to Sarah to tell her the tea was ready.

Sarah emerged from the bedroom, her blouse and skirt back on,
 and moved sleepy-eyed toward the table.
Raymond poured tea for both of them and said:

274

I've got a confession to make. From the beginning, Sarah,
I felt something special, more, just for you.

You mean, even before Ann died.

Yes. It just happened. Oh, god, how I lusted for you!

You've had the hots for me for ten years?

Yes.

Sarah stared at the steaming surface of the tea inside her cup.

This is so stupid, Raymond. It's just stupid for me to be living
two miles down the road all alone and you living here alone too
when we both feel the way we do about each other.
Why don't you come live with me. I've got lots of room,
and it would be nice, for both of us.

Do you mean it?

I do.

I couldn't. As much as I might want to,
I couldn't leave this place. My whole life has been this place.
I'm rooted here. It would hurt too much to pull myself up.

It's only two miles down the road, for God's sake.
That's pulling yourself up?

Yes.

You're right. It couldn't work.
You're too stuck. It could never work.

Sarah got up from the table and began moving toward the door.

Maybe it could. We could try it, just try and see.

Are you serious?

Yes. Only,
how about you move in over here with me?

You sneak.

V

Sarah moved in with Raymond and discovered very shortly—
within a couple of weeks—that she was not as desperately lonely
as she had once imagined. She discovered within herself
a contentment, a peace and an independence
that must have been there all along.

And so it was that Sarah, while giving Raymond all the love and
    assurance she could, left him
and went back to her own place and thereafter each of them
    maintained his and her own independence and privacy,
yet engaged in a loving and intimate conjugality as well.

They looked after each other, often taking their meals together,
    occasionally spending the night together,
making love and working together.

And this is how they passed their days through the end of
    that summer and fall and into that winter.

All this took place without the town knowing much about it.
Edith, of course, wagged her tongue as much as she could,
but both Raymond and Sarah were so discreet and reclusive that
    there was little to gossip about.

The truth is,
in small and remote towns like Judevine it is not remarkable
    what the town's folk know about each other's lives,
it is remarkable what they don't know.
The degree to which we all live our lives in real isolation from
    each other is overwhelming
and really not that different in the country from what it is in the
    city.
What we know of each other, no matter how much we may think
    we know,
is nothing compared to what there is to know.

Some people find this isolation from each other
a terrifying fact of our condemned and modern lives.
Others find in it a kind of privacy and solitude
without which they could not survive.

RAYMOND KILLS A DEER

Halfway through November.
Toward evening and raining.
At the meadow's edge:

low
brown
sudden

hawk. Hunter. She
who is terror to those who shudder against the earth
moves in silence

through the gray rain.
Feather soft she moves,
cold and soft,

her talons hung beneath her
limp
as broken fingers.

That night the first snow falls and whispers against the windows:
Raymond. Raymond!
Come out of your house and kill again.

He twitches in his sleep,
in his dream he sees
a bloody carcass steam and drip.

Out in morning dark he pushes through the new snow
watching the ground,
picks up a track and follows, then

strikes off tangentially, slides across the sidehill
and circles broadly away from
what he thinks is the buck's intention,

settles under a hemlock
on a ridge of maple, ash and beech
and waits, shivers, in the dawn.

Below him, a brown spot behind gray trees.
Raymond watches down blued steel.
The buck takes a step, waits.

His eyes scan the hill,
only his ears up, pricked forward,
move.

The shot resounds three miles across the valley
strikes a ridge, returns. The deer goes down,
then rises and is gone.

He slants down the sidehill on three legs
drawing a red line
behind himself.

Seven o'clock.
Raymond will watch the drip
of this life,

follow this
unraveling thread
all day.

Off the hardwood ridge, through cedars and swamp,
over a softwood knoll, across a brook and on,
never faster than he has to, keeping just ahead

of his assassin, the murdered beast flees and bleeds
on fallen logs and withered ferns, dragging
his shattered leg through the new snow.

Across a pasture, into the sugarbush, through a sag,
down a logging road
and on.

Here, at the brook where the buck drank,
Raymond dips down, drinks too, and rests;
eats his lunch. His sandwich tastes like blood.

Later, further on, where the buck rested:
the red, red, bright red snow
packed from his ragged shoulder.

He who is dead
is dying.
Yet he goes on.

Now Raymond sees him just ahead bounding into thick spruce.
More blood now
waist high on branches, more and more.

Then, under a wind-felled naked maple,
finally,
the killer and the killed.

Raymond pulls the hammer back and finishes
what he began
nine hours earlier.

The buck shivers;
his mouth foams blood;
his eyes bleed.

Twitch, twitch.
Twitch.
Twitch.

Quick
and simple
as that.

Raymond sits at the murdered head,
strokes the murdered neck
speaks softly words of comfort.

He rolls his sleeves.
Knife in at the sternum
slices to the anus.

He dumps the steaming stomach and intestines on the ground,
cuts away the diaphragm, extracts the lungs, the broken heart,
puts the liver in a bag.

Where life was,
a hole gapes.
Fat shimmers white in blood and bile.

Off the ridge now, in the dark, he comes,
bloody to the shoulders, dragging,
two hundred pounds of deer.

Red-faced, sweating
he moves through the cold
and starless night.

From where the rear hoof scrapes the woodshed floor
to antler tip—eight feet—this creature stretches,
hung.

Raymond! Supper.
I'll be right in, Ann.
Don't be long.

Raymond leans against the woodshed door
and wonders for a moment why he took this life.
He knows the gutless carcass does not die.

He knows this winter it will rise again and run
down long red alleys through another misty wilderness
around his bloody heart.

But what his mind can comprehend is not enough.
There are too many lives in this life,
too many deaths,

and no amount of thought can save him from his grief
for dying things, not even knowing
resurrection,

sure
and green
as spring.

✦

Raymond steps inside his house,
removes his boots and overclothes,
washes hands and face at the kitchen sink.

He sits down at the telephone and sighs:
Hello? Sarah?
I've killed a deer.

Could you come over,
help me butcher it?
There'll be enough for both of us.

ENVOY TO RAYMOND AND SARAH AGAIN

Raymond and Sarah sustained their life together and at the same
    time maintained their independence from each other through
    that late fall and into the winter.
They shared Christmas, looked after each other through the dead
    of winter and when the light hovered longer in the southern
    sky, they started plants together.

Sometimes we'd stay over at one or the other of our places,
only usually, almost always actually, at Raymond's,
he didn't want to leave his place for much of anything,
you know how he was over there. He was a tree.

We didn't always sleep together, in spite of what the gossips said.
All they ever think about is sex.

There's more to life than getting laid.
Mostly we almost never spent the night together;
we didn't have to since we both liked making love best
in the afternoon. Anyway, no matter what, if I wasn't over there
when morning came, I'd call him, every day.

Mud time came and went and spring was coming on.
It was a warm, dry spring that year, I remember, the kind
we almost never have around here, a nice one, not too much rain,
just enough. You could put your plants out almost every day
to harden them and lots of nights you didn't even have
to bring them in.

I called him that morning. When he didn't answer, I knew.
I thought about calling someone to go over with me.
I was afraid. I didn't want to see him that way—alone.
But I couldn't think of anyone I knew well enough
to want to have them there with me when I went in.
I mean, you know how everyone, especially the women,
disapproved of us. Besides, after a little while I knew
I wanted to do it alone. It was just the two of us
when we were both alive, so why not just the two of us
now that one of us was dead?

He was at the kitchen table. He just slumped forward, face first
onto the table. He was lucky, so lucky to die that way.
He didn't suffer. He just dropped dead. He wasn't even sick.
That's the way I want to die.

Sarah made the arrangements for the funeral
which was held toward the middle of May.
A tiny handful of people came.

REQUIEM FOR A HILL FARM

Raymond died last spring.
Or was it fifty springs ago?
It doesn't matter.
It was spring.
It is always spring.

A warming day. Winter's back
broken. Light rising.
He quit. Gave up
the ghost. Left
a withered carcass slumped
across the kitchen table.

With the man gone
the place dies
like an old pine dying
bit by bit, from tips
inward. The outward sign
of inner forgotten death.

The garden goes to witchgrass, timothy,
aster, hardhack,
gray birch, red maple.
Balsam, spruce begin
their long reach through the roof
of his old car.

One night coyote sits
on Raymond's porch
and howls: notice to the rest:
this again
is nowhere.

Mullein grows
midroad.

The roof lets in rain.
Joists buckle, floors warp,
rafters groan and sag.
All give up geometric pretense,
go pulpy soft.

Chimney brick dilapidates.
Someone steals the windows.
Porcupines come in.

The house fills with quills and shit.

Two dead porkies in the sink.
The sofa is a nesting bird's delight.
A broken chair.

Then down.
Disheveled nest.
Pile of sticks.
There is no in   no out.

Raspberries sprout from Raymond's
sodden mattress.

What boards are left turn black.

WHAT REALLY HAPPENED

That's the way it happened in my dream, the way I wish it would
     have been—
that little spot in these wooded hills, a croft cut out of forest
     momentarily,
now reverting still again, back to the way it was before they came.

But the way things happen and the way we wish they would
are almost never the same.

Here's what really happened.

Distant relatives of Raymond's in Pennsylvania somewhere
    inherited the
place and, having no interest in it, put it up for sale.

Late one moonlit night,
not long after Sarah got wind of what was happening,
she drove to Raymond and Ann's, got out of the car,
opened the trunk and removed four plastic wash basins,
a five-gallon pail and a shovel.
She went to the perennial gardens and dug up a clump of gloriosa
    daisy, some phlox, some Siberian iris and a couple shovelfuls of
    delphinium, and put each into a basin,
then put the basins in the trunk.
Next she went into the garden and began going about from place
    to place digging shovelfuls of soil and putting them into the
    five-gallon pail.
When the pail was full, she put it in the trunk also,
put the shovel in and drove home.

Very early the next morning Sarah planted the perennials in her
    own flower garden,
then took the bucket of dirt and emptied it by portions
into a shallow basket which she then cradled in her left arm
and went about over her own garden
broadcasting Raymond and Ann's soil onto her own.

Not long after that, Raymond and Ann's sold to a real-estate
    developer who immediately made plans for condominiums.

First, however, the developer cut out a parcel that included
the house and barn and a few acres.
It sold almost immediately.
Forty years of detailed care, upkeep and attention,
had made the place a gold mine in a market

286

glutted with abandoned and collapsing farms.

Then the surveyors returned, laid out and staked the lots and roads
    for the condominiums and
the bulldozers moved in.

SARAH'S NEW FRIEND

Sometime early that summer Raymond and Ann's farm
got cut up for lots, there was suddenly
a young man staying at Sarah's place.
If Sarah by now was forty,
this new guy couldn't have been more than thirty.

By the middle of the fall, Sarah was obviously pregnant
and the gossips' tongues wagged again saying:
Finally!
and:
It's about time she found a man who could work that thing
to make it do what it's supposed to do!

To which Edith countered that that just couldn't be since
she'd heard he was a veteran of Vietnam and because
of that he was sterile, that he had got his insides changed around
or something. Something about having gotten sprayed
with Agent Orange. She didn't know the details.

Others said that Edith had to be all wrong
since he was just too young
to have been in Vietnam.

✦ ✦ ✦

GRACE AGAIN

It was three years between the time Grace came up
to give me Tommy's poems and when I saw her next.

I had just pulled in to Jerry's, gotten out of the car and was headed
into the store, my head down thinking about something, as Grace
was coming out. She saw me first.

Oh! Hi, David. Hi.

Well, I'll be. . . . Hi, Grace. Boy, it's been a long time.

Yes, it has.

My gosh, it is nice to see you.

It's nice to see you too.

How you doin'?

Good. Real good.

That's terrific. I'm really glad to hear that.

I got a new boyfriend now.

Good. That's terrific.

We been goin' together, let's see, must be, hell, since
last winter sometime anyway. I was workin' as a chambermaid
down to Stowe, at the Edelweiss, you know. He always stays
at the Edelweiss when he comes up to Stowe.

That's terrific.

Yeah, and it's workin' out good too. He's good to me
and good to the kids too. He always brings us presents,
the kids and me, I mean.

He's got money?

Oh, David, he has got pots of money. I mean, David,
he is rich. Like you don't know.
He runs an import business in New York, or somethin',
I don't know what it is, but, I mean, Mister, he is rich!

He's got an apartment in the city, up on the Upper East Side.
    Eighty-third Street.
It looks out over the East River, 34th floor, and, I mean, big too!
With big floor-to-ceiling windows that look out on to the river
    and across to Queens and Brooklyn.
God, the Brooklyn Bridge is so beautiful at night.
The Queensboro Bridge is too, that's the one right close to where
    we live,
but not so much, not so much as the Brooklyn Bridge.

I just love to stand at those windows after the kids are all in bed
    and watch the river and the lights and all the lights reflected in
    the river.
I never thought I'd like New York, but it is beautiful!

Yes, Grace, I know. I used to live there.

Well, ah . . . that's right . . . isn't it? I mean . . . then you know . . .
how beautiful it is . . . I mean . . . at night . . . with the lights.

Yes.

Of course, he won't let us come while the kids are doin' school.
He says my kids have got to get their educations.
He's very big on education.
He's good to them. I mean, he really cares for them.
You lived in New York, didn't you?

Yes.

But when the kids are out of school, he sends his plane right up
    here to Burlington.
He's got a private plane and a private pilot too.
He sends his plane right up here to Burlington and we drive in
    and meet it.

Grace, please.

We fly down to La Guardia and his chauffeur and his limousine
    picks us up
and takes us right up to the door of his apartment building.
I mean, is that good or what? How can you beat that?

You can't.

He's also got a place down in the Caribbean. It's a little island,
he owns the whole damn thing, off one of those bigger islands,
I don't know which one.
He's got some kind of mansion, a chateau,
a private beach and everything. He says the water is so clear
you can see clear to the bottom right down through sixty feet.
I haven't been down there to that one yet,
but we're all going down come wintertime this year.
He says he's getting sick of these Vermont winters
and he's also getting sick of Stowe. Well, shit! I said yes to that!
You can imagine what I said to that!

He says to hell with skiing and to hell with Stowe.
He says we are all
going to the Caribbean this winter, about the first of December
is what he said. I'm going to take the kids out of school
and we're all going down there for the winter.
He's going to get the kids a private tutor.
He's already got a housekeeper and a cook down there.

He's really big on education. He says my kids have got to get
an education so they don't end up like me and have to spend
their whole lives working by the hour down to Stowe.
I mean, he is big on education.

That's good.

Oh, Jesus! Look what time it's got to be. I got to go.
Every afternoon about this time, he calls me on the telephone.
No matter where he is, he calls me on the telephone.
If he's in the limousine he calls me on the mobile phone.
He always wants me home to get his call. I got to go.

David, it's been nice to see you. How you been?
You still livin' up there on the hill? I got to go.
It's been nice to see you, David.
I wish I could talk a little longer,
but he calls me every afternoon. I got to go.
Take care, David.
It's been nice to see you.

She turned from me, stepped off down the road,
saw someone else,
went up to them and said:

Hi. Hi. I got a new boyfriend now. It's workin' out good too.

What?

I said, it's workin out good. He's good to me.
Good to the kids too. . . .

✦ ✦ ✦

SARAH'S BOY

Eight years now since Raymond died. December and time again
for the Judevine Elementary School Christmas Open House and
     Exercises.
I saw Sarah and her son, who is now a third grader, together there
     this past December.
From all I can observe, he's a good-natured boy,
with an unusually delightful sense of humor,
and quite tall for his age, angular and bony,
and he has this odd cackle when he laughs.

The night of the open house I saw him come running up to Sarah
with his chum, a kid named Sam, and he was saying, almost
     shouting:
Mom! Mom! This is my best friend in the whole world.
This is Sam!
Do you think he could sleep over sometime soon?

Sarah said hello to Sam and that she was glad to meet him
and also said of course he could, that would be fine,
just set a date and we can do it.

Then Sam and little Raymond sauntered off into the crowd,
their arms around each other.

Later that evening I saw Sarah talking awkwardly with a woman
     who I took to be Sam's mother.
She wore a white uniform and she looked hard and tired.

WHAT I HEARD AT
THE DISCOUNT DEPARTMENT STORE

Don't touch that. And stop your whining too.
Stop it. I mean it. You know I do.
If you don't stop, I'll give you fucking something
to cry about right here
and don't you think I won't either.

So she did. She slapped him across the face.
And you could hear the snap of flesh against the flesh
halfway across the store. Then he wasn't whining anymore.
Instead, he wept. His body heaved and shivered and he wept.
He was seven or eight. She was maybe thirty.
Above her left breast, the pin said: Nurse's Aide.

Now they walk hand in hand down the aisle
between the tables piled with tennis shoes
and underpants and plastic bags of socks.

I told you I would. You knew I would.
You can't get away with shit like that with me,
you know you can't.
You're not in school anymore.
You're with your mother now.
You can get away with fucking murder there,
but you can't get away with shit like that with me.

Stop that crying now I say
or I'll give you another little something
like I did before.

Stop that now. You'd better stop.

That's better.
That's a whole lot better.
You know you can't do that with me.
You're with your mother now.

THE END IS THE BEGINNING

Down at the junction of Routes 15 and 100 there is and has been,
for the past ten years, a new town slowly growing.
They paved over two hundred acres of meadow and in it now
we've got a couple quick stops, four gas stations, two supermarkets,
a hardware, three video rentals, a discount department store,
two banks, two auto supplies, a pizza parlor, a fancier restaurant,
a paving contractor, a video game arcade, a florist, an optometrist,
a paint and carpet store, a lumberyard and, just last year
our very first McDonald's.

I was in the discount department store looking for some spray
to kill a nest of yellow jackets who had decided to homestead
inside the woodshed right where we all needed to pass by.
I finally found someone I hoped could help me:
a bony girl about eighteen,
drooping mouth, gapped teeth, sloe eyes, and a look of boredom
so intense and terrible I wanted to run away.

From her pierced ears dangled cross-of-Jesus earrings
and another cross hung from a necklace between her breasts.
Because she wore a sleeveless blouse I could see on the outside
of her left shoulder where her vaccination scar should have been,
a tattoo that said: Jim.

I told her I needed wasp and hornet spray and she said she had no
   idea where such a thing would be or if they even had it,

but suggested I try health and beauty aids.
After I didn't find it there she suggested sporting goods
and climbed down off the stool she'd been slouched upon,
came out from behind her little counter and led me toward
the basketballs and swim fins.

She wore loose flats, no socks or stockings,
and she shuffled when she walked so that her shoes
made a rhythm out of scrape and clack
as she moved across the floor.
We didn't find it there either.
She turned to me blankly and said: Sorry.
Then she shuffled, clacked back to where she'd been.

As I left the store and began to weave my way through the forest
of asphalt and parked cars, someone sitting in a car behind me
said:
Shitagoddamn! I ain't t'ink I see you again
'til we bot' be togedder on da odder side!

Antoine climbed out of his car and we hugged each other
and held each other, patted each other's back and began to visit.

Oh, it is nice to see you, David, how you be?

Then Antoine pulled his head back the way a boxer does to avoid
    a jab,
cocked his head and said:

What's dat white dere I see in your hair above your ear dere,
    David?
You been workin' on your house and get some pain' in it?
Wall, I know, I been pain'in' my house too.
An' I see you los' your beard too, an' I know why you can't find
    it,

'cause you like me, I know you be, you don't want da wimens see
you got white pain' all aroun' your face too.

Wall, you know . . . no, you don't—how could you be?—you
    ain't been up our way in so long—
we got our new double-wide manufacture' home,
an' she's as beautiful as a house she could be. I wish dat you could
    come up sometime
an' see it, an' us . . . an' us in it too.

We leaned against his car, folded our arms across our chests and
    visited
until Antoine proposed we walk up to the new McDonald's
and have some pie and coffee.

Come on, let's go, I ain't been in dere yet. Besides, I got naut'in'
    else to do
'til Shirley an' Michelle come oudda dat store and pro'bly dat be
    tomorrow or nex' week.
I'll just leave a note here on da dashboar' an' den dey can come
    on up dere an' join us
if we still be young enough by da time dey get dere.

We crossed the rest of the parking lot, entered McDonald's
and stood in line until it was our turn to put our order in.
The girl who had been my guide at the discount department store
    had somehow gotten herself out of that store, across the parking
    lot, into a McDonald's smock and behind the counter,
and all that in the time it had taken Antoine and me to walk half
    that distance,
and she was now taking our order for pie and coffee.

I said Hi but she didn't recognize me.

You know dat girl?

I thought I did.

She remind me of my high-school sweetheart fifty years ago.
She was da nicest girl—I mean da one I knew fifty years ago,
I don' know dat one—you'd ever wan' to meet, but her face
be one only a mudder could love, an' as far as I know
dat's da on'y one what ever did.

We found a table next to a window that looked out
on an expanse of asphalt and four or five hundred cars
and Antoine looked around both inside and out and said:

Wall,
dis ain't be da wild lot up on Stannard Mountain where we see
dat snake wid legs or Doc's pond where we catch does trout—
you remember dat time, David?— or much like wearin' rain suit
and eatin sand'iche outinda snow under a bully spruce tree
early in December, by Jesus don't you know.
Times change an' we did too. Wall, what else is dere to do?
Make it new, David. You got to make it new.
Good coffee.

Antoine told me about how he quit working for Bert not long
    after I did
and took a job as a janitor at the high school over in Hardwick,
and how that was a good job until he hurt his back and got laid
    off and then retired.

An' you remember my baby, Michelle? Wall,
I know you won't belief it but she be a soph'more naow
down to da college and majorin' in French and English literture.
Says she iss gonna be a poet! Bah gosh, David,
I dunno where dat came from.

It came from you, Antoine!

I don't see how dat could be. Anyway, naow I got a betty coed
livin' in da house wid me! A college girl, can you imagine dat?
An' Shirley, she say she iss gonna go to college too, says naow
since I'm retire', I can stay to home, cook and sew.
Wall, you know, I don' mind. So I keep da garden
and mow aroun' da place nice an' haf flowers,
like I never used to haf da time to but always wanted.
I like to be at home all day, an', David,
you know how I like to cook.
So naow I got college girl, emancipated wimens an'
I'm gonna be a housewife too.

We gossiped about everybody we could think of, had another
couple cups of coffee, then Antoine changed the subject and said:
I hear on da grapevine dat you make a play
outta your poems and stories,
an' I hear you pud me in it too.

It's only someone like you, Antoine.
No one could ever copy you.

Wall, I know, it mus' be awful hard doin' what you do.
You know, David, it's funny. All da years we know each odder
an' I never read a word you wrote. Ain't dat funny?

Wall, someday maybe I could see dat play, see myself
up dere on da stage, only I dunno if I could stan' it.

Antoine looked at his watch, then out the window toward his car:
What can dey fin' to look at in dat place for all dis time?
I might grow old an' die before dey get into dat checkout line!
I got to go see what de're doin'.

We left McDonald's and I walked Antoine back toward
the discount department store. I promised to come see them

and their new double-wide manufactured home and we said
  good-bye.

I watched Antoine walk into the discount department store,
then I got into my car and looked out through the windshield
across the parking lot and access road to the edge
of what was left of the 200-acre meadow, a little corner of a field
cluttered now with abandoned tractor-trailer rigs,
once used for temporary storage, but now useless and rusting,
sprouted there on the edges of the asphalt as naturally it seemed
as milkweed or mullein in a wasted place beside the road,
and the tractor-trailer rigs surrounded by a chain-link fence,
someone's notion of security for these discarded artifacts
of goods and motion.

I could see the inevitable hole in the fence
and I imagined the path
leading from the hole to the back door of one of the rigs.
Edith, I have heard, claims the local kids go in there
and "shoot dope" as she puts it.

Then I saw him, standing near the hole, his fingers hooked
into the fence and he staring into the enclosure.
He couldn't have been more than twelve.

Two older kids came along
and there was some kind of altercation among the three,
some words. Then one of the older kids
pushed the twelve-year-old to the ground.
The two older boys bent down,
slipped through the hole in the fence and disappeared
into the back of one of the abandoned semis.
The little kid got up,
hooked his fingers momentarily into the fence again,
then released the fence with a *thwang,*

300

turned away and started down the service road
past the pizza parlor toward the asphalt plant
where I saw him cut through a vacant lot,
climb over some mounds of paving rubble and disappear
among the delivery trucks and dumpsters
at the back of the shopping center.

I started the car and drove home.

✦ ✦ ✦

AFTER TWENTY YEARS

Dawn: another summer morning
and I am sitting on the porch with my tea, the grass wet,
the sunlight through the dew-wet spiderweb in the apple tree,
the pileated woodpecker calling in the near distance,
the ravens calling far away,
the garden yawning, drenched:
spreading its myriad and various leaves
toward another day.

The farmers on the hills and in the bottomland,
what farmers there are left,
and there are almost none,
are already doing chores.

Down in Judevine village everything is quiet, but soon Conrad,
who is still around, will pad the hundred feet from home,
unlock the garage, turn out the light in the window that says:

Beer

put on the coffeepot, turn on the gas pumps and the air
    compressor and then
stare out the window
at the empty, early morning road.

Soon also, Roy McInnes, he's still at it too, a mug of coffee in his
    hand, will move from house to shop,
swing open the doors of doors
and begin another day.

Edgar Whitcom and Laura Cate, both of them retired,
in their separate houses, will rise, prepare their separate breakfasts,
and go about the things they do to get ready for the day.

Alice died a couple of years ago and her lover, who never was
    interested in junk, had an auction,
then sold the place and moved on.
Now the mill is empty,
but I heard just the other day that a young couple, from away,
had bought the place, said it would make a nice restaurant.
They'd put a deck out off the back, you know,
so you could sit and have a drink and watch the river.

The condominium development over on Raymond and Ann's
    land has gone bust.
They put in the roads, built a couple units and quit.
Nobody's living in them and the weeds are beginning to grow
in the middle of the road.

Just two miles down the road from there, off in an isolated corner,
hidden, almost invisible, as if they were living underground, Sarah,
who is fifty now, and her constant friend of these past ten years,
seek a way to continue, to survive.

Sam and Beatrice Hines endure, and they remain good-natured,
kind and stately, their long suffering and loving kindness
an inspiration to us all.
Sam and I are going fishing come September,
up on the upper Lamoille.

I haven't seen Grace in years.
I'm not even sure if she still lives around here.
Maybe she's moved on to someplace else.

There are plenty of us who have.
Arnie went back to Massachusetts.
Bobbie and Doug lost the farm and got divorced and each of
    them moved away in different directions is what I heard.

Anson and Marie left Burlington and nobody's heard about them
    since.
Lucy finally got sent to Waterbury which is where she died.
And Jerry—remember Jerry?—he dumped his middle-aged wife
    and ran off to New Jersey with a twenty-two-year-old girl.

Edith had a field day, told everybody:
I could see that one comin' a mile away!

And there are those who moved to the other side, so many ghosts:
Raymond and Ann, Granny, Lucy, Alice,
Charlie Ketter, Tommy, Cyd.

Summer wanes and fall comes on.

Twenty years in this place.
What seems real one moment is fiction the next
and gone out of existence the moment after that.
Nostalgia is the greatest enemy of truth,
and change our only constancy.

No matter who lives, who dies, the seasons never rest.
Creatures take their turns, and the year turns and turns.

November again.
The earth is dank and chill as an old deserted cellar.
The bare trees, their skinny fingers darkened by the rain, stretch
against the sky.

The sky is empty. The birds are gone.
Dark. Darker still. And winter coming on.

The sky steals light from both ends of the day.

Four o'clock. Almost dark.

Roy McInnes closes the doors of doors
and stands for a moment in the evening
watching streams of commuters going home,
then he too turns and goes home.

Down at The Garage,
Conrad turns on the lights above the gas pumps,
turns off the air compressor, sits down in a chair
and begins the evening
as he has for twenty years:
beer and blackberry brandy.

And winter coming on.

DRIVING HOME AT NIGHT

Midnight. Outside the car it is
fifteen below. A foot of new snow.
The village is deserted, dark,
except for eight streetlamps
and the light in the window
at Jerry's Garage that says:

    Beer

The smell of woodsmoke seeps
into the car.

Judevine, ugliest town
in northern Vermont, except
maybe East Judevine.
Disheveled, wretched, Judevine—
my town—is beautiful in the night.

It is beautiful because
its couple hundred souls
have given up their fears,
their poverty and worry.
For a few hours now they know
only the oblivion of sleep
and the town lies quiet
in their ease.

INDEX OF TITLES